WALKING ON WATER

WALKING ON WATER

Knowing Your Purpose in God's Perfect Plan

Alfredo Martinez Jr.

WinePress Publishing (PO Box 428, Enumclaw, WA 98022) functions only as book publisher. As such, the ultimate design, content, editorial accuracy, and views expressed or implied in this work are those of the author.

ISBN 1-57921-779-6
Library of Congress Catalog Card Number: 2004118350
Printed in Colombia

TABLE OF CONTENTS

Introduction vii

Chapter 1: Walking on Water 11

Chapter 2: Walking with God 29

Chapter 3: Walking in Understanding of God's Perfect Plan 47

Chapter 4: Walking in God's Perfect Will 67

Chapter 5: Walking in the High Call of the Spirit 95

Chapter 6: Walking Deeper in Victory 123

Chapter 7: Reason Drowns the Hearts of Men 147

Chapter 8: Walking Epistles 175

Chapter 9: Walking into Spiritual Warfare 201

Chapter 10: Walking in Newness of Life 225

Source 247

INTRODUCTION

Walking on Water is designed to help you to understand God's purpose for your life and to show you how to fulfill it as easily as breathing God's air. Receive these spiritual truths, and you will be able to run your course with the strength of a trained athlete. God has great things in store for you.

It took twenty-five years for me to understand *spiritual* concepts. When I understood them, I began to fulfill God's calling on my life. I became unstoppable. I know these truths will enlighten your life also. I pray that with time you may take these truths to the next level of your life and your relationship with God.

I hold to all the teaching of the ministers before me with deep reverence. I agree with all the teachings of the Christian church. For years, ministers have studied the Bible to learn what people should obey. However, I give practical details about *how* and *why* to obey, not just *what* to **obey.**

I grasped the torch from almost 2000 years of Christianity—spiritual knowledge that has been handed down to me—and I ran with it.

The central reason that people disobey God's Word is that they do not understand how or why to obey. If God's people know how to obey him, this understanding will help them to please God. My life is dedicated to understanding *how* and *why*. Spiritual knowledge guides people into the right path. Spiritual knowledge is a weapon of spiritual warfare.

This book was born when my bank account was empty, when I did not know how in the world I was going to make the next mortgage payment. God taught me the deepest spiritual truths when He took from me the things that I held dear. God shook my cute Christianity to the core and made me look at the Bible as a life preserver, not as a read-along, sing-along book anymore.

I have never seen an angel or a demon or heard an audible voice of God. Everything I have learned, I discerned by meditating on the Bible and in prayer with the help of the Holy Spirit. This book is solely for the advancement of the kingdom of heaven. I now pass the torch of spiritual knowledge on to you.

The difference between many previous Christian authors and me is this: I admit that I am human and very capable of error. I just discovered something so profound that I want to share it with you. However, if another generation comes along and proves me wrong (only by the Word of God) then let me be a liar and God be true. If someone else discerns a more godly way, then let me be a liar and God be true. Nevertheless, I have carefully studied the Bible all my life and my conscience bears witness that I am on the correct path. I know in my heart that this book is for my generation now.

Every Christian book was written for the enlightenment of their generation. Its purpose should always be to advance the kingdom of heaven—just like medicine, technology, or any secular field is advanced by every generation's discoveries. One generation improves on the other. So it is with the Christian kingdom. Every Christian generation should pass the torch of spiritual knowledge to the next generation.

As you read this book, I encourage you to read the Bible verses and follow along. So, get out a Bible—the most-sold book in history—and study with me.

Money-Back Guarantee

This is the first Christian book that I know of with a sixty-day money-back guarantee. If this book fails to make an impact on your life, mail me the receipt; keep the book, and I will refund your money. I put my money where my mouth is. One condition is that you read the entire book before requesting a refund. What do you have to lose? Are you an atheist or non-Christian? I dare you to read this book from beginning to end. I challenge you to be open to other viewpoints. Isn't that a secular thing—to be open to everything and every viewpoint? Come on, take up my challenge.

I have faith that the Word of God is quick and powerful and does not return unto God void. I place my faith on God's Word and therefore I give a sixty-day guarantee.

For a refund, mail your receipt of purchase and a stamped, self-addressed envelope to:

Pastor Alfredo Martinez Jr.
PO Box 524
Gridley, CA 95948

On the other hand, if this book has enlightened you, and you want to send a love offering and prayer requests or invite me to speak to your Christian group, please do so.

Love,
Alfredo Martinez Jr.

Chapter 

WALKING ON WATER

And in the fourth watch of the night Jesus went unto them, walking on the sea. And when the disciples saw him walking on the sea, they were troubled, saying, It is a spirit; and they cried out for fear. But straightway Jesus spake unto them, saying, Be of good cheer; it is I; be not afraid. And Peter answered him and said, Lord, if it be thou, bid me come unto thee on the water. And he said, Come. And when Peter was come down out of the ship, he walked on the water, to go to Jesus. But when he saw the wind boisterous, he was afraid; and beginning to sink, he cried, saying, Lord, save me. And immediately Jesus stretched forth his hand, and caught him, and said unto him, O thou of little faith, wherefore didst thou doubt?

—Matt. 14:25–33

In this famous biblical passage we have a mind-blowing account of Jesus walking on water. Then to make the incident even more awesome, Peter asks Jesus to let him walk on water, too. Jesus replied, "Come." It boggles my imagination that somebody like you and me actually walked on water.

When Peter walked on water, he entered into a new world. A strange world that defied logic and physics. Peter was accustomed to the physical laws of gravity as we all are. But now he was defying the law that he had taken for granted all his life. Now, a new law was at work, a law that kept his body from going under.

Peter's five senses screamed at him that his actions were physically impossible. Then the physical world claimed his attention as the wind and the waves began to rise. The physical overwhelmed his mind so much that Peter doubted the power of Jesus' word, and he began to sink. Although Peter did walk on water for a couple of steps, his mind could not believe he was actually doing it. His mind was not accustomed to this phenomenon, so his mind could not comprehend it.

What laws were at work here? If Albert Einstein would have set his mind to analyzing the spiritual laws that make up the universe, his findings would have had more of an impact for eternity than his findings on other subjects. Peter later became an apostle who understood these spiritual laws and walked strongly in them. He learned to live in the world of God where all things are possible.

Peter and the other apostles were full of the spiritual manifestations of God, but now they are gone, and here you are. There is no difference between you and Peter except for understanding. Once you understand spiritual laws, your eyes will see like never before. Your chains will fall off. You will know the truth, and the truth will set you free. By the time you finish reading this book, you will proclaim, "I am free. I am free! Whoever the Son sets free is free indeed!"

I believe the church will apply spiritual truths. I believe the church is seeking these answers. I know they are. Once it is revealed, the church will walk in them and be strong in them. The world will stand in awe at the power that will be manifested in us and through us. This is our destiny. Our time has come. God is pouring out great wisdom and grace. Every day we shall find deeper understanding in the Spirit.

In Daniel 12:4, Daniel prophesied that in the last days knowledge shall increase. This knowledge not only refers to technology, medicine, or other secular fields but also to spiritual knowledge. This spiritual knowledge will allow us to discern how to bring God into our lives and how to walk with him as God desired it to be.

The only knowledge that will do you any good in this life and in the life to come is spiritual knowledge. Spiritual knowledge has definitely increased. Now we have computers, the Internet, and cable television. We can spend hours and hours researching spiritual information or listening to preachers. God will hold our generation to a higher standard of accountability because of all the information that is at our disposal.

Where is the power of God in our churches today? At one time people touched God and had great revivals where the five-fold ministers were born with great conviction and anointing. (Note: Term "five-fold ministers" refers to apostles, prophets, evangelists, pastors, and teachers given by God for the edification of the church, Eph. 4:11.) But now we have lost the spiritual truths that gave us power from God. We've lost the keys to access the throne of God. He did not run out of power. He is still the same God of power and miracles.

Any minister who claims that the power of God ended with the apostles is spiritually ignorant. Any denial of the power of God in us today is a lie of the Devil, no matter who says it. Ministers who deny God's power are deceived. Jesus says the same thing to them as he said to the ministers of his day: "Ye do err, not knowing the scriptures nor the power of God" (Matt. 22:29). "Making the word of God of none effect through your tradition" (Mark 7:13).

The grace of God did not stop. There were not more miracles available back then than there are today. God's power is all around us. God's grace is all around us. The Glory of God is all around us. Salvation is all around us. God's abundance and healing are all around us. These blessings cannot come down from heaven. They are already here.

Jesus finished his work on the cross and sat down at the right hand of the Father. Now it is up to us. Wake up, and realize that if we do not have power, it is because we are doing something wrong, or we are following the wrong path.

I love faith preachers and the faith movement, but faith is only the foundation. Wake up, Faith People. Faith alone is not power. If it were, then why does the Bible say that we must add unto our faith (2 Pet. 1:5)? Miracles alone are not power, nor speaking in tongues, nor gifts of the Spirit, nor any fruit of the Spirit. The Bible says that the Spirit was upon Jesus. That alone is power.

Let us begin to learn the ways of the Spirit. When we totally focus on faith in our lives, we only want to prosper. However, when we want God's Spirit, we focus on his work in our character. That is a major key in this story of life.

Is the power of God for us, today? Yes. When you finish reading this book, you will understand how to grow in God's power. I know you may have doubts. I know chains of sin may bind you. They bound me, too. But then the power of God came into my life and anointed me to be a teacher. By the grace of God I can now teach you as well.

God did not mean for his children to live without power. On the contrary, God wants them to live with his glory, grace, and power. Life is impossible without them. Marriage is impossible without them. God meant for you to walk in power and grace. Grace to obey God. Grace to love. Grace to humble yourselves before God. Grace to minister. Grace to do everything.

Jesus lived with great grace and so must we. Jesus grew strong in the Spirit and was filled with wisdom because the grace of God was upon him (Luke 2:40). Jesus was full of grace (John 1:14). Jesus spoke with grace (Psalm 45:2, Luke 4:22). This grace of God is now available and is provided to us by Jesus Christ (1 Cor. 1:4). Jesus will teach everyone the exceeding riches that are in God's grace (Eph. 2:7). Jesus has made us heirs of God's grace (1 Pet. 3:7). God is able to make all grace abound toward us as he did his son, Jesus (2 Cor. 9:8,14). Now, like Jesus, we must grow in grace (2 Pet. 3:18), be strong in grace (2 Tim. 2:1), and be established in grace (Heb. 13:9). Also, like Jesus, we must speak with grace (Eph. 4:29; Col. 4:6).

This book will also teach you the *hows*, and the *whys* of grace, so that you may soon say with Paul, "But by the grace of God, I am what I am; and his grace that was bestowed upon me was not in vain; but I laboured more abundantly then they all: yet not I, but the grace of God which was with me" (1 Cor. 15:10).

You and I are so alike. We are made up of intellect, emotions, and feelings. We may look differently on the outside, but we are alike in our inward being. We might share the same fears: such as the fear of poverty, the fear of pain, or the fear of losing a loved one. We share many insecurities. We bear the same feelings of distrust and hate.

We are so alike because God fashioned all of our hearts from the same essence (Ps. 33:15; Gen. 1:26). We even look for the same things on this earth—peace and happiness. Nevertheless, the more we seek to be happy, the more we seek money, the more we seek pleasures, the more we seek safety, then the more we will feel empty. Why is that? This question has taken me into a journey seeking these answers. At last I figured it out. I will explain to you in detail these truths that have taken me so long to understand.

Whether you are a Christian or not, this book will give you powerful spiritual truths that will change your life. This book will answer your greatest questions. You can find that which you seek most—peace and happiness. Do not harden your heart until you have finished this book. Do not criticize me until you have finished this book.

What you are about to understand will take you into the world of God. Slowly, you will learn to depend less on your ability, reasoning, emotions, feelings, and desires. You will begin to depend totally on God. You will be walking on water.

As all walks, this journey starts with one step. In the physical world you could not walk when you were born. You were weak but grew strong with the milk that your mother fed you. Several months later, you stood up and took some steps. It is the same in the spiritual world. You are born again by accepting Jesus Christ as your personal Savior. You become strong in your faith by the milk of the Word (1 Pet. 2:2). Now you should walk on your own, but here is where many Christians are stuck. I know because I was a Christian infant for twenty-five years.

Do not expect to put down this book, kneel in prayer, and have the power of God fall on you. That is the way of reasoning and of the flesh. No, the things of God are not cheap. And it is only his way or the highway. His way is a walk: not a run, not a sprint. God is not concerned about what you can do for him with his power. God is first concerned about what his power can do for you.

When the disciples saw Jesus walking on water they were troubled because walking on water is impossible. The disciples became afraid because they assumed that what they saw was a ghost. When they cried out, Jesus told them not to be afraid. "It is I," he said. In spite of Jesus' assurance, the disciples still could not believe their eyes. Peter said, "If it's you, let me come to you on the water."

This is why God only reveals himself a little at a time. Our minds cannot handle God in the beginning stage of our Christian lives. Our life must be a walk because our understanding has to be renewed. As the Holy Spirit states in Romans 12:2, "Be not conformed to this world, but be ye transformed by the renewing of your mind, that ye may prove what is that good, and acceptable, and perfect will of God."

As the disciples began to walk with Jesus and hear his words, their understanding of God began to be renewed. More importantly, their view of their lives and their purpose in this present world also began to be renewed. They saw Jesus raise the dead, heal the sick, and walk on water. They saw Jesus stop the storm. Then they asked with great fear, "What manner of man is this that even the wind and the sea obey him?" That is where God wants you, where you ask a spiritual question.

You are reading this book because God has brought you to a point in your life were you are asking a spiritual question. Does God exist? Can God help me? Can God fill this void in my life? How can I get hold of God? What is God's plan for my life? Can God deliver me from sin? The answer is yes. I will show you how.

The time for you to walk with great wisdom and power has come. This is the day that King David proclaimed, "Thy people shall be willing in the day of power . . ." (Ps. 110:3). Another great spiritual discerner was Daniel. He wrote, "But the people that do know their God shall be strong and do exploits" (Dan. 11:32).

When you begin to walk on water (enter into a new relationship with God) you will begin to change. Your family will notice the grace of God that has come into your heart. Be a spiritual pioneer in your family, your church, your community, at work, and to all nations. The Spirit of God is more willing to walk with you then you are to walk with him.

The more we walk with God the more we trust him with our lives. The more we trust him with our lives, the more he trusts us with his power and wisdom. This is your destiny. The more we trust and depend on God, the more we trust and depend on his grace and wisdom. We begin to understand that something far greater than the physical laws of this world sustains our life.

What holds us on top of the water? The same thing that holds the universe together: the power of God's Word. Hebrews 1:3 says, "Who being the brightness of his glory, and the express image of his person, and upholding all things by the word of his power . . ."

Jesus told Peter, "Come." One word from Jesus had the power to hold Peter on top of the water. Just one word from Jesus and the physical laws have to obey the spiritual laws, always. Just one word and God's power will confront all we know. One word. The physical world recognized the voice of its Creator. Soon you, too, will recognize the voice of your Pastor, the Good Shepherd, Jesus Christ.

The only thing Peter had to do was to trust in that word. Peter saw his spiritual leader walk on water, but that was not enough to hold Peter up. Peter had to depend totally on the word of Jesus. Peter's dependence on that word would have held him up. However, Peter doubted and began to sink. If anything can shake our faith, we will sink.

When Peter felt himself going down, he cried out. Jesus stretched out his hand and said, "Why did you doubt?"

Do you have any doubts? Let's deal with them once and for all. Leave your doubts behind and step up to a new level in God, where everything you do comes from an established foundation of faith.

I don't have any doubts in my God. I nailed them all to the cross, and I have never looked back. I'll help you jump this hurdle.

Soon, you will awake in the morning excited about experiencing God. Instead of simply wondering if there is a God or wondering if life has any meaning. You'll arise in the morning rejoicing that, "This is the day which the Lord hath made, we will rejoice and be glad in it" (Ps. 118:24).

If the Devil can shake your faith in the existence of God then you cannot soar to higher levels with God. However, once I prove to you that God exists, then move on once and for all in your life. Move on in the name of Jesus Christ. Move on, my brothers and sisters.

Proof of the existence of God

Can your mind comprehend the existence of God? If I were to prove to you the existence of God, would you surrender your life to him? Would you raise other questions? Would you reason God out of your mind? Either way, it always comes down to your own personal choice. I am praying that your heart may be open enough to allow some light inside.

For many reasons, we know that God does exist. Order does not come out of chaos. A watch does not come into existence without a maker. So it is with the existence of man, who is by far more complicated than a watch.

Scientific atheists argue that the universe had a beginning in the Big Bang theory. There is a problem with this concept or any concept that tries to prove that the universe began without the help of God. Order and harmony does not come from an explosion. An explosion does not bring into existence wisdom or life.

The basis of the theory of evolution is that with vast amount of time, complicated structures build upon simple structures. The physical world is not improving or evolving through time but the opposite is occurring. The physical universe is breaking down with time and use just as the Bible declares (Isa. 51:6). This Big Bang theory, although their best theory so far, is ridiculous.

Here is another problem with the Big Bang theory: What was out there before the Big Bang? What substance was it made from? Where did that substance come from? Everything has to have a beginning. However, this is something the reasoning men of our time do not understand. What the scientific world is desperately trying to prove is that the physical begat the physical. They forever try to solve the riddle of ***what came first, the chicken or the egg?***

In the beginning, the physical did not give birth to the physical. The physical did not come from the physical. The physical cannot create the physical. This is what the scientists are trying to prove and, as you can see, it cannot happen. There will always be this question with man-made theories: where did matter come from and what existed before that?

NASA can send up hundreds of space probes in hope of finding answers about the origin of the universe. There are no answers in space but more questions. The only thing they will find in space is the handiwork of God.

Scientists and intellectuals who are trying to figure out the mystery of the universe are like dogs chasing their own tails. They can study all the books they want. They can receive all the degrees and diplomas they want and act very intellectual all they want. Nevertheless, in trying to prove the origin of the universe without putting God into the equation, they are simply running in circles.

These scientists want us to believe that the entire universe came from something smaller than a grain of sand. How can the sun alone come from a grain of sand? This is what they are selling to our children in our greatest universities. They are selling the Brooklyn Bridge to our kids who do not know how to question these intellectuals.

The only conclusion we can find to the *where, why,* and *how* questions about the origin of the universe is that something that is not physical made the universe. This is something our minds cannot totally comprehend. A power outside physical boundaries and outside of time made the universe. That power calls himself *God.* He relates to our reasoning in a way we can understand, yet often our minds cannot handle God's simple truth, and we reject it.

I have to give some credit to those evolutionary scientists. They are on the right track. The creation of the universe did begin with a Big Bang, and light energy did go forth. The Big Bang was God's spoken word, "LET THERE BE LIGHT!"

What substance did everything come from? Faith. God had faith in his own words: "Now, faith is the substance of things hoped for, the evidence of things not seen. . . . Through faith we understand that the worlds were framed by the Word of God, so that things which are seen were not made of things which do appear" (Heb. 11:1,3). Faith is more real than the physical universe. Faith lives in a different dimension, yet everything we see was made by God's faith in his word. "In the beginning God. . . . And God said. . . . And it was so" (Gen. 1).

Why do our minds reject the concept of God? Our minds were made to understand and interact with the physical world. When it comes to God and spiritual matters, we can only relate to him and please him through our hearts.

Our minds are not capable of believing in God. Our minds will always seek for proof. Our minds will only believe what we see, feel, hear, smell, or touch. Even if we see angels or miracles, our minds will find a way of reasoning them out of existence. Our minds cannot believe, only our hearts. Jesus said in Mark 8:17, "And when Jesus knew it, he said unto them, why reason ye, because you have no bread? Perceive ye not yet, nor do you understand? Have ye your heart hardened?" "For with the heart man believeth unto righteousness; and with the mouth confession is made unto salvation" (Rom. 10:10).

Do not allow your mind to bind you to the physical world, which is only temporal. Do not allow your mind to keep you from God's joy, righteousness, and peace. The only thing that keeps you from God is your unrenewed mind. Your mind and spiritual matters are always at odds. Something has to surrender, God or your mind. I have news for you, in the end God does not lose. "Because the carnal mind is enmity against God: for it is not subject to the law of God, neither indeed can be" (Rom. 8:7).

The worst thing a human can do is harden his heart towards spiritual truth. Only through the heart can our Creator reveal himself to us. Israel and the Jews have suffered so much because they hardened their hearts towards spiritual truth. That is what the Bible teaches. It also teaches us not to harden our hearts like they did (Heb. 3:5–8).

Could it be that simple? Yes, everything about us and about God is that simple. God has revealed himself to us on simple terms. You will be amazed at how simple it is to enter into your destiny with God. Jesus Christ himself said that one must become as a child to enter into the kingdom of heaven. We must have child-like qualities such as trust, faith, love, and meekness, like a child trusts his father. The things of God are so simple. Our doubts and reasoning complicate everything.

Do you still need more proof of God's existence? OK, how about Bible prophecy? Old Testament prophets foretold Jesus Christ's entire life. These writers lived more than five-hundred years before he was born. What about Bible prophecy regarding the end times in which we live? There are many Christian books out there on this subject. Please read them. Only God knows the time. Much of Bible prophecy has been fulfilled, is being fulfilled, and will be fulfilled. We are so close to the end of time that most Bible prophecy has been fulfilled, and the rest is being fulfilled before our very eyes. God knows what he is doing. He knows all time. He is the Alpha and Omega, the beginning and the end.

Then there is proof of God's existence through testimony of people. I heard an atheist ask the question, "If God exists, why doesn't God part the Red Sea?" If God would part the Red Sea, and the atheist saw it, the atheist will still find a reason to doubt God exists. I would respond that the mere existence of Israel as a nation is a testimony of God's power. If the Red Sea had not parted, Israel would not exist today. Israel still celebrates their liberty from Egypt through the Passover that they have celebrated from generation to generation even until now.

What about the testimony of those who have had a near-death experience, went to heaven, and came back? Countless people have testified to this occurrence. Dr. Raymond Moody left his occupation as doctor and spent time recording reports of patients who experienced this. He was the first to coin the term "near-death experience." He has written several books on the topic including, *Life After Life*. You can read his book or other books written about near-death experiences in bookstores or surf the web on this topic.

You may say this phenomenon is all subconsciously induced. Well, what about those stories about people who left their bodies, then came back and repeated everything that was said in his room, or a man who described objects on the roof of the hospital? Somebody climbed on the roof and confirmed his story. These things are true. The mind cannot grasp it, but open your heart.

Want more proof? How about the million of miracles that go on around the world that give God the glory and doctors are dumbfounded. Medical doctors now say that prayer has an incredible effect on physical illness. In many medical journals they now encourage families to pray for their loved ones.

Want more proof? OK, what about our conscience? If evolution is correct, there would be no a need for a conscience. According to evolution, only the strong and wise survive. However, when we try to live according to their ideals, we feel guilty, out of place, and empty. Where did this conscience come from? From God who placed it in our hearts to guide us. "Which shew the work of the law written in their hearts, their conscience also bearing witness, and their thoughts the mean while accusing or else excusing one another" (Rom. 2:15).

Want more proof? What about archaeology that is proving the Word of God correct every day. What about one of the oldest cities of the world, Jericho, discovered with its walls broken down from a force pushing them outward instead of inward as in a usual battle—just as the Bible says. Who broke those walls? The power of God. You can study all these new discoveries on the Internet. Come out of your box, and look at the world.

Do not harden your heart against God. Do not say like the Pharisees said to Jesus, "Show us a sign!" Do not say unto God, "Prove to me that you are God!" What more proof do you want? Look around you. Information about God is everywhere. Evidence of the existence of God is all around you.

Why did God choose to reveal himself to our hearts and not to our minds? First of all, he is God. In other words, he is the one who makes the rules. If we are wise, we will follow them and prosper spiritually, mentally, emotionally, physically, and financially on this earth. He reveals himself to our hearts because our hearts are the only things in this universe that are made up of the same spiritual stuff as God. I say *spiritual stuff* because I am not able to explain this organically or chemically, not by anything physical.

Our heart is our spirit-being that God made in his image. When God breathed on Adam, man became a living soul. When the spiritual touched the physical, a third element was created: our souls. We are one being, composed of three elements just as God is composed of three: Father, Son, and Holy Spirit. We are a spirit that has a soul that lives in a body.

Our spirit-being was made to have a relationship with what Native Americans called the Great Spirit. Our soul is our intellect and our emotions. Our body is corrupt by nature. It is not eternal but is the temple or housing of our spirit and soul. Our soul is not meant to guide us. Our spirit guides us through fellowship with God.

God gave our hearts a free will to choose. This is what God cannot control. He can influence our spirit but cannot control our wills. If we *will* to open our hearts to him, he will come in and sup with us (Rev. 3:20). If we choose to reject him, there is nothing he can do but continue to offer spiritual knowledge to persuade us to open our hearts to the truth.

God gives us the option to obey him. If we choose to disobey him, there is nothing he can do. Think about it. If we choose to close our hearts to him, he cannot help us. The moment that we begin to seek him, we have the beginning of wisdom. All God can do is provide us with spiritual truth. It is up to us to open our hearts to the truth.

However, when you are exposed to spiritual truths, there is an anointing that will help you. There is so much power in spiritual truths that will draw you in more and more. You will want to drink more and more from that fountain. After reading this book, you will not be the same. You will be a new creature. You will be born again by the power of God's grace and mercy.

God has called us to walk on water. Are you ready to come out of the boat?

Chapter 2

WALKING WITH GOD

And if ye call on the Father, who without respect of persons judgeth according to every man's work, pass the time of your sojourning here in fear.

—1 Pet. 1:17

After Adam, few understood the spirit of a sojourner—an awareness that life in the physical body in a physical world is temporal. Few men have stopped to completely understand the purpose of their existence. Few men have ever scrutinized their lives to understand the meaning of life. Few men in history have ever put on the spirit of a sojourner and learned its wisdom. Now, your time has come to be a part of those few and walk with God.

Throughout history, God showed men this spirit of a sojourner: Enoch glimpsed this and begin to sojourn with God until he just walked into heaven (Gen. 5:24; Heb. 11:5).

Job also realized he was a sojourner in the land and said in Job 1:21, "Naked came out of my mother's womb, and naked shall I return thither: the Lord gave, and the Lord hath taken away; blessed be the name of the Lord."

In Genesis 6:9–22, God told Noah why and how to build an ark. God told Noah to get inside the ark with his family in Genesis 7:1. God shut the door of the ark, but God never told Noah where the ark was going. Noah and his family had to develop the spirit of a sojourner. They trusted God while it rained, while they waited for the waters to dissipate, and while they waited to find their final destination

In the same way, God spoke to Abraham and told him, "Get up and go out of your country." God never told him his destination either, but Abraham took on the spirit of a sojourner and trusted God with his life.

> *By faith Abraham, when he was called to go out into a place which he should after receive for an inheritance, obeyed: and he went out not knowing whither he went. By faith he sojourned in the land of promise, as in a strange country, dwelling in tabernacles with Isaac and Jacob, the heirs with him of the same promise; for he looked for a city which hath foundations, whose builder and maker is God.*
>
> —Heb. 11:8–10

Abraham did not question God but obeyed him with a meek heart. Isaac and Jacob understood the spirit of a sojourner and lived in tents. They didn't build homes or cities because they knew they were just passing through. They understood that life on earth is temporal and that their final dwelling place would be a heavenly city that was created by God.

Moses embraced his destiny as a sojourner in the land. He fled from Pharaoh, leaving behind his wealth and title. Did he ever desire to return to Egypt (Egypt symbolizes the world and sin), and call Pharaoh's daughter, *Mother*? Not for a moment (Heb. 11:24– 27). He became strong in this spirit of a sojourner. When Moses's first son was born, he named him Gershom which means, "I have been a stranger in a strange land" (Ex. 2:22).

King David understood the spirit of a sojourner and wrote a psalm that expressed his heart. ". . . for I am a stranger with thee; and a sojourner, as all my fathers were" (Ps. 39:12).

Have you caught the spirit of a sojourner, yet? Catch it, and be strong in it. We are sojourners in this land. Our days are numbered on this earth. We are eternal beings in a temporal body. We are not going to live forever in this physical world. When you catch the spirit of a sojourner, God will begin to show you what is important on earth and what is not.

Pride makes man foolish and blind. Pride gives birth to selfishness and vainglory. The father of pride is the fallen angel Lucifer who is now Satan, the Devil. He teaches man how to be temporal instead of eternal. Man fights for lands, material possessions, and wealth. Like Cain, men kill out of selfishness, greed, and envy. They think they will live forever. They ignore the truth that it is appointed for men to die once and after this to stand before God in judgment (Heb. 9:27).

John the Baptist came along, and the spirit of God was strong in him. He came out of the desert preaching, "Repent, for the kingdom of God is at hand." Jesus Christ, My Lord and Savior, was led to the desert by the Spirit. He, too, came out preaching, "Repent, for the kingdom of God is at hand!"

God's Spirit also leads us to the desert of our souls so that he can teach us new spiritual truths. Understanding spiritual truths will make an impact on our lives. In time, we too will come out of that desert proclaiming truth. The truth of God never changes. Once it enlightens us, the truth changes our being.

One truth that no one can dispute is that life is temporal. If we are then temporal, let us embrace the spirit of a sojourner and please God with our lives.

"Vanity of vanities, all is vanity" (Eccl. 1:2). The only thing that is worthwhile on this earth is living righteously by doing God's will. When God teaches you this truth and you become strong in this truth, you, too, will come out of the desert of your heart. You will preach and proclaim, "Repent, for the kingdom of God is at hand!"

Come on, Reader, reason with me. Let me stretch your thinking. What is important for you? Your goals and desires? Your education and career? Your family and work? Your house and bank account? Your reputation as a smart and good person? These are all good things.

Twenty-five years from now, what will be important to you? What about fifty years from now? What about one-hundred years from now? Your children's inheritance? The incredible political changes you brought about? The inventions that made life more delightful?

What about one-million years from now? What would be important? What about when the human race no longer exists on earth? When the earth burns up? What would be important then? Nothing, My Friend, is more important than doing the right thing in the eyes of your Maker.

King Solomon, the wisest man, realized that all was vanity. He concludes his book of Ecclesiastes with these words, "Let us hear the conclusion of the whole matter: Fear God, and keep his commandments: for this is the whole duty of man. For God shall bring every work into judgment, with every secret thing, whether it be good or whether it be evil" (Eccl. 12:13–14).

What was important to Jesus Christ while he was on earth? Was it a piece of real estate? Money? Power? Influence or prestige? That all men should respect him? His own glory? Acceptance from the government, from fellow ministers, or his followers? The only thing that was important to Jesus was doing the exact will of the Father. He did not speak of himself, but he spoke of the Father. He did not speak his own words but the words of the Father. He did not glorify himself, but he glorified the Father.

Temporal men fight to control and dominate people's lives. Jesus Christ came to serve men and set them free. Temporal men do the works of the Devil while Jesus Christ came to destroy the works of the Devil. Men kill and die for lands, riches, honor, and pride. Jesus Christ came to die not for temporal things but for eternal things of great value, even our souls.

Jesus Christ had the spirit of a sojourner. While the Jews wanted a Savior to establish an earthly kingdom, Jesus spoke of a spiritual and heavenly kingdom that was of his Father. He taught with parables about the kingdom of God.

In the kingdom of God there is eternal life. If anyone accepts God as his Lord or King then the Kingdom of God will be established in his heart, and he will have eternal life (Luke 17:21). He taught us that the kingdom of the Father has greater value than an earthly kingdom. He encouraged us to establish treasures in heaven and not on earth, for where your treasure is there will your heart be also.

Where is your heart? What is your goal in life? Remember that eternal life is far greater than anything else. "For what is a man profited if he shall gain the whole world and lose his own soul" (Matt. 16:26)? If our final destination is the grave and then heaven, why not use our time for eternal benefit rather than waste precious time on the temporal?

Listen, Reader, do you believe in life after death? Why or why not? On what do you base your beliefs? Because somebody said so, and you believe that somebody? You'd rather believe a spiritually ignorant man with diplomas than God manifested in the flesh who healed countless people and rose from the dead? After two-thousand years his prophesies are still being fulfilled.

God has placed a conscience within you. You know that there is a right and a wrong. You think it's a coincidence that you have that knowledge in you? It's no coincidence. God gave you a conscience to help you discern his ways.

Jesus tried to convey this attitude to all the people who heard him, rich people particularly because it would be hard for them to enter the kingdom of heaven (Luke 18:24–25). A rich young man approached Jesus and asked how he could obtain eternal life. Jesus answered, ". . . if thou wilt be perfect go and sell that which thou hast, and give to the poor, and thou shalt have treasure in heaven: and come and follow me . . . the young man went away sorrowful for he had great possessions" (Matt. 19:16–22).

The young man preferred earthly possessions rather than eternal life. When possessions grab the heart, that heart finds it difficult to understand spiritual things. It was not the possessions of the rich young man that were wrong but his attitude.

You must understand the spirit of a sojourner. "Seek ye first the kingdom of God and all these things shall be added to you" (Matt. 6:33). Our faith and dependence should not be on earthly things but in God. This doesn't mean that material possessions are evil, or that we should live in poverty. On the contrary, this means that we should make God and his standard number one in our lives. Then he will prosper us and give us what we need. Still, letting go of material possessions is not the main point. We must follow Jesus Christ into eternal life.

It is hard for the rich man to be meek. It is hard for the rich man to see others better than himself. It is hard for the rich man to humble himself before others. With his natural wisdom, he has gained wealth and this has given him an earthly sense of superiority to others. He dresses and eats better than others. He has people serve him. He thinks because of his financial wisdom he has the right to be lord of the masses. Money has become the god in whom he trusts. He feeds off the power and influence that money gives him. He has become proud and, therefore, useless to God, useless to humanity, and useless to heaven.

The Word of God says, "Ye have lived in pleasure on the earth, and been wanton: ye have nourished your hearts, as in a day of slaughter" (Jas. 5:5). In other words, the rich man has fattened himself like a pig, and he is ready to be slaughtered on Judgment Day.

"For whosoever exalteth himself shall be abased; and he that humbleth himself shall be exalted" (Luke 14:11). Therefore, be wise. Humble yourself now, so you may be exalted in heaven with a crown of life and enjoy eternal life as a ruler with Christ. If you exalt yourself now, you shall be humbled in hell with the father of pride and lies, the dragon and deceiver of nations. The decision is yours. You have been given the ability to choose. Be wise and put on the spirit of a sojourner. Accept the things of God with a meek and grateful heart.

Jesus Christ used parables to teach people about the kingdom of God. Yet, the people of that day didn't understand because the physical things were too important to them. They had ears but could not hear. They had eyes but could not see. Their hearts were calloused, so they could not understand spiritual things.

The parables of the kingdom of heaven can be broken into three categories:

Who can enter the kingdom of God?

Through many parables, Jesus Christ taught that the time would come when we will all stand before God, and the righteous will be separated from the wicked. Some parables teach that some people worked harder on earth than others, but all the faithful will inherit life. Some served and knew Jesus Christ as their Lord and Savior for more earthly time than others, but all who have Christ will inherit the kingdom. Also, he who has the heart of a child will enter—a heart that meekly obeys the Father with complete trust.

How can one enter the kingdom of heaven?

Jesus taught that the kingdom of God suffered violence, and the violent take it by force. Through parables like the hidden treasure, the lost coin, and the pearl, Jesus taught that one should consider heaven more important than anything else. One should dedicate himself wholly to seeking God. Our desire should be him. Our thoughts and our hearts should desire to please him.

How important is eternal life to you? Are you willing to obey Jesus completely to obtain eternal life? Become violent in the spirit and answer, *Yes! If I have to carry my cross and humble myself, I'll do it! If I have to love my enemy, I'll do it! If I have to submit to all authority for God's sake, I'll do it!* Be violent with the things of God. Be aggressive in love, meekness, peace, and righteousness. Let your spirit be powerful against yourself. Self is your only true enemy. Deny yourself so that you may be worthy of eternal life. Eternal life is worth it!

What happens to you when the kingdom of God is in you?

Jesus taught that the kingdom of heaven is like a mustard seed. It is small but when it grows, the seed becomes a great tree. The kingdom of God is like leaven (yeast). When a baker works yeast into the dough, the whole dough ball becomes leavened.

These parables teach that when the message of the kingdom of God is shared and when it enters our hearts, it is small at first, and we're not strong in it. We don't quite understand it, but with time it will grow in us. We must meditate on the kingdom of God, nourish the tree, and work the leaven into the dough until the things of God grow strong in us, until obeying God becomes natural. When God reigns in our hearts, the cross becomes a blessing, not a burden. We count it all joy to suffer for the kingdom. When the kingdom is strong in us, we will bear fruit.

Finally, there are parables that teach us about the King of the Kingdom. He is merciful and just. His greatest quality is that he loves us and with open arms he waits for us to choose the right path. Day and night he worries about us, hoping that we will listen to our hearts and return to him. His love for us is beyond measure or understanding. He loves everyone without exception.

Through the Holy Spirit, the disciples (now apostles) learned the spirit of a sojourner. They all understood that life on earth is temporal. Therefore, they devoted themselves to the cause of Jesus Christ. The truth was established in their hearts.

Peter wrote, "For all flesh is as grass, and all the glory of men as the flower of grass. The grass withered, and the flower thereof falleth away" (1 Pet. 1:24).

John wrote, "Love not the world . . . and the world passeth away, and the lust thereof; but he that doeth the will of God abideth forever" (1 John 2:15–17).

Paul wrote, "I have fought a good fight, I have finished my course, I have kept the faith: henceforth there is laid up for me a crown of righteousness, which the Lord, the righteous judge, shall give me at that day: and not to me only, but unto all them also that love his appearing" (2 Tim. 4:7–8).

James—the brother and a servant of Jesus Christ—wrote, "Whereas ye know not what shall be on the morrow. For what is your life? It is even a vapour that appeared for a little time and then vanisheth away" (Jas. 4:14).

All these New Testament men had a deep understanding of the spirit of a sojourner. They conveyed this spirit throughout their lives and writings. However, they no longer called it the spirit of a sojourner, but the New Testament name for it was *the hope of the glory of God.*

The Bible tells us to rejoice in the hope of the glory of God (Rom. 5:2). God is hope. He fills our hearts with joy and peace. The Bible tells us to abound in hope (Rom. 15:13). We should work in hope and be partakers of his hope (1 Cor. 9:10). The eyes of our understanding should be enlightened, that we may know what is the hope of his calling and the riches of the glory of his inheritance in the saints (Eph. 1:18). We should constantly be thinking on that blessed hope (Tit. 2:13).

The hope of our salvation is the helmet in the armor of God. Hope guards our thoughts from being earthly minded (1 Thess. 5:8). The people of this world have no hope. They are prisoners of fear and depression. Suicide is their way out. Their souls are deeply despondent, and they have no hope to soothe them. The Scriptures teach us to lay hold of this hope, the anchor of our souls and to be strong in it (Heb. 6:18,19).

Do not underestimate the power of hope just because you do not understand it. Hope is just not sitting around waiting to die and go to heaven. Hope gives us direction in life. It puts our priorities in perspective. It gives us a clear picture of why we are here on earth and what we must do.

When hope is revealed to our hearts, we conform our lives to the gospel of Christ. We are careful to obey it in its fullness.

Hope should not be a theory or a mental idea, but it should be alive in us. Hope should not be a passing thought. It should be a stone in the foundation of our thought and character. "Which according to his abundant mercy hath begotten us again unto a lively hope by the resurrection of Jesus Christ . . ." (1 Pet. 1:3).

Hope gives us the wisdom to realize that one day we will be in heaven. Someday, we will all stand before God. Therefore, hope orients our faith so that we can believe the promises of God, not for ourselves or our desires but for the advancement of the kingdom of heaven. Hope gives our faith direction so that we may understand that we are not placed on earth to accumulate riches for our egos but to use riches for God's glory.

Hope does not have much need of material possessions. Who cares whether somebody has a bigger house or car or career or bank account? I have eternal life. What else do I need? Can I take my earthly materials to heaven? No, but I could sure take my soul and other souls! Souls! Souls! That is what God is interested in.

Be established in God's hope, and wisdom will be given to you that is far greater than the wisdom of all the great business men or political people of the earth. They have a temporal perspective, but we are eternal beings. They are shortsighted, but we can see their vanity and their folly and their end.

If you understand the power of hope and allow it to flourish within you, your thinking will change. The way you feel about the things of this world will change. Life is temporal. The only thing that matters is to please our Creator. "And every man that hath this hope in him purifieth himself, even as he is pure" (1 John 3:3).

Is this hope alive in your heart? Or is it just in your thoughts? Today, you know about this lively hope because you read it, and it made a slight impression on you. Nevertheless, tomorrow you will go to work and the godless people at work who are around you will convince you to forget the hope that is in you.

Dear Reader, I pray to God that you will clearly understand what I am trying to say. Let this hope come alive inside of you! Burn with its understanding. Meditate on heaven until heaven and hell are more real than this puny temporal life. Let the reality of hope overcome the lies of hopeless people around you. Be strong in hope. When you see hopeless people, you will see their coming future as cast out from the presence of God. Let your spirit rise up within you along with a great need to witness the gospel and relentlessly say with great compassion, "Repent, for the kingdom of God is at hand."

Pray to God that he will reveal eternity to your heart. Do you have any idea what eternity is? I am sure you know the word, but it is only an abstract concept. Establish your heart in hope and you will understand that eternity is forever. There will be no end.

Meditate on what eternity is. Ask the Holy Spirit to give you insight into what eternity is. When you understand what eternity is, the fear of the Lord will come upon you. Eternity is just too long for us to take the things of God lightly. The things of God were never meant to be taken lightly. They are serious. They are life and death forever. Whether your fear of God is a respectful reverence or just plain terror, let it result in wisdom. Seek God that you may inherit such a wonderful gift as eternal life.

When we live with hope, and it is strong within us, we can easily witness to anyone. No matter what influence or social level people are in, we can share the blessed hope that is in us. ". . . and be ready always to give an answer to every man that asketh you a reason of the hope that is in you with meekness and fear" (1 Pet. 3:15).

The world sees Christians as narrow-minded people. Do you think I know nothing about life? Do you think that I read my Bible and go to church just to be a goody-goody Christian? No, I seek God in my life because he holds my eternity. I seek God because I know the imminent coming that is before me. I know that I will stand before God, and he will judge me. Everything within me knows that I will die. The conscience that he has placed within me will testify for me or against me (Rom. 2:15–16). That is why I urge everyone—especially my most cherished family—to seek God and think about the great picture of life.

The world is selfish. The world enjoys the creation but never considers the Creator who made it and gave it life.

Their only goal in life is to satisfy themselves. They have no purpose but to serve money, their stomachs, or their fleshly desires. This creates a spiritual void in their being. Without an understanding of God, they will perish.

Whom do the dwellers of this earth run to in time of trouble? Soon they will not run in fear, frustration, and desperation to the atheist, the evolutionist, the scientist, the comic, or the government looking for hope. They will turn to you, the Christian. They will ask the church why you have peace and joy while their lives are falling apart. You must be ready to give an answer for the hope that is within you.

This hope in Christ Jesus becomes an answer to a godless, sinful, captive world.

New-Testament men turned the world upside down in their time. They laid hold of this hope. They had a meek heart before God and considered life on earth to be an opportunity to do something for the glory of God. These men are no longer here, but you are.

What are you going to do for God? The time will come when you stand before him. Then you'll see the great men of the past, and they'll ask you, "What did you do for the glory of God?"

Hope gives us the strength and desire to work for God. Every Christian should be established in hope and give themselves to the work of the ministry. My fellow Christian, there is nothing else worthwhile on earth. To help God save a person from eternal damnation is the greatest task given to the church. What an awesome responsibility!

God has chosen to preach, heal, flow, live, and walk through human vessels like you and me. The world is looking to the church for help. They are yearning to know that we have the wisdom and the power to help them. The world is not looking for an emotional answer or a smart answer, like psychology. The world needs to know the reality of the hope that is so strong within us. "To whom God would make known what is the riches of the glory of this mystery among the gentiles, which is Christ in you, the hope of glory" (Col. 1:27).

In heaven God will no longer need us to help him reach souls with his message. God needs us to reach souls now. We seek God for his grace to accomplish this task. As long as we are in this physical body in this physical world we will strive to work for God. Once hope is established in our hearts, we desire to do things that please God. The time will come when we will not need his spiritual gifts because we will be with him. Now, let us put on the armor of God and go to battle. Now, let us grow in the knowledge of Jesus Christ. Now, let us work and labor for our God. Now, let us believe in our God for marvelous things.

God is waiting for you to lay hold of this hope and become his son or daughter on earth, to become one of his generals. My Bible-school president used to quote, "If God has called you to be his minister, don't stoop down to be an earthly king."

My heroes are people like Mother Teresa, Rev. Martin Luther King Jr., and everyone who is involved in helping the poor and sick. My heroes are people who live selfless lives. My heroes are people who put others before themselves. These are the people I admire and desire to emulate. These are the people who allow God to establish hope in them.

If you are going to live once on earth, are you going to live selfishly? If you are going to live once, are you going to live like a coward? Are you going to worry only about your desires and future only? If you are going to live only once, live for God and let your life count!

If you are going to live only once, let the hope of God rise up within you and say, *God help me see the true meaning of life. Help me to live an unselfish life. Help me to be brave and stand on your promises!*

Do not let negative prophecies of God's Word be true in your life.

> *This know also, that in the last days perilous times shall come. For men shall be lovers of their own selves, covetous, boasters, proud, blasphemers, disobedient to parents, unthankful, unholy, without natural affection, trucebreakers, false accusers, incontinent, fierce, despisers of those that are good, traitors, heady, highminded, lovers of pleasures more than lovers of God.*
>
> —2 Tim. 3:1–4

Let hope rise up within you that God may also say of your life, "Of whom the world was not worthy!" (Heb. 11:38).

The time has come for you to sojourn in this land and walk with God.

WALKING IN UNDERSTANDING OF GOD'S PERFECT PLAN

Remember the former things of old: for I am God, and there is none else; I am God, and there is none like me. Declaring the end from the beginning, and from ancient times, the things that are yet not done, saying, my counsel shall stand, and I will do all my pleasure.

—Isa. 46:9–10

God is a spirit. He loves all the noble qualities. In contrast, we do not completely understand what is just and noble. We cannot trust our hearts. Our hearts can deceive us. We can always trust God's spirit to leads us to obedience to his Word.

God is eternal. He lives outside of time. He never had a beginning, and he will never have an end. Can there be other gods like him? He assures us that he is the only God. If God says he is the only one, then he should know.

God reveals himself to man in three manifestations: the Father, the Son, and the Holy Spirit. How can God be revealed in three persons? This is a stumbling block for the Jewish religion. My human mind is constantly trying to understand this truth. The Bible agrees that it is a mystery. "And without controversy, great is the mystery of godliness: God was manifested in the flesh, justified in the Spirit . . ." (1 Tim. 3:16). "In the beginning was the Word, and the Word was with God, and the Word was God" (John 1:1). "For there are three that bare record in heaven, the Father, the Word, and the Holy Ghost: and these three are one" (1 John 5:7).

When God made the universe and set it into motion, time was created. He is the author of time and knows all time. He is the only one who will bring time to an end (Rev. 10:6). Within time he has created dispensations. In every dispensation God has a plan for man. Man focuses on himself and on the present time, but God wants man to focus in the great scheme of things. Do you know what time it is? This is the dispensation of grace (Eph. 3:2).

God made us in his own image and after his own likeness (Gen. 1:26–27). To me, this verse means we have great potential in all of us to do good. One meaning that is widely accepted in all Christian churches is that we are spirit with the ability to have God's noble qualities. In fact, he made us so that he could teach us these noble qualities, but time after time, man has followed ways that are empty and deceiving.

Our flesh is not made after the likeness of God, but our spirits are. Jesus Christ became man so he could experience what we experience. Jesus Christ conquered the flesh and the law of sin. He paved the way of wisdom and power so that we are more than conquerors in him (Rom. 8:37).

Man followed sin and ate of its fruit. He enjoyed only that level of understanding. Soon man became a slave of sin. He fell under the bondage of emptiness. As sin came into the land by one man, Adam, so victory over sin came by one man, Jesus Christ (Rom. 5:12-21).

Before God made man, God made the angels. They were created to minister and serve God's will. One angel named Lucifer began to think something that was not allowed. Angels were allowed to meditate only on the things of God. They were not allowed to contemplate anything outside of God because that would be a lie.

Lucifer means *light*. He was a beautiful angel. Because of his beauty, pride rose in his heart. We do not know how long he dabbled in this new realm of pride, but we know that eventually it began to poison his heart. He should have taken this thought to the obedience of Jesus Christ, but he loved pride. Finally, he said in his heart, "I will ascend into heaven, I will exalt my throne above the stars of God . . . I will be like the most high God" (Isa. 14:12–15).

Lucifer tried to pervert the will of God by trying to establish another will. We know that Lucifer preached his new doctrine to other angels until one third of them followed him. We do not know how many angels precisely, but there were a great number of them.

If Lucifer was able to deceive those holy beings, how can man stand against his deception? If he could deceive these holy angels who knew God's presence and saw his glory, then it is no wonder that he can deceive the nations.

There is no salvation for fallen angels. God cannot have grace upon them because a spiritual law states that it is of faith that it may be by grace (Rom. 4:16). Angels knew God face to face, in a way that man cannot comprehend. They knew eternal wisdom in a way man can only imagine.

Angels were made knowing God, but man was born not knowing God. Angels could see God, but John 1:18 declares that no man has ever seen God. Therefore, if any man has faith in God because he heard the gospel, then God will have grace on him for salvation. Jesus said, "Blessed are they that have not seen, and yet have believed" (John 20:29).

Likewise, when any man dies, his time of faith for grace is over. His true self is a spiritual body that one day will stand before God (1 Cor. 15:44). When he beholds God with his spiritual body, there is no more faith, and God can no longer have grace upon him. After physical death, the dispensation of grace is over, and the dispensation of judgment has begun. That moment will be so awesome that Jesus Christ declared, "There shall be weeping and gnashing of teeth . . ." (Luke 13:28).

Lucifer (now Satan) tells man to take pride in himself. This leads to self-exaltation. This message will lead you far from God. Jesus Christ tells man to humble himself and practice self-denial. This leads him to the grace of God. The only thing we can use to fight the deceptions of the Devil is our knowledge and understanding of the Word of God, like Jesus did when the Devil tempted him. Jesus told him, "It is written . . ." (Matt. 4:3–11).

God created the heavens and the earth. After some time, he created animals—even the dinosaurs (Ps. 104:26, Job 41:1–34). The catastrophe that made dinosaurs extinct may be when God cast Lucifer and one third of the angels out of heaven. Jesus said that he saw Satan hit the earth as lightning (Luke 10:18). That is when Satan hit the earth and shook God's creation to its core. The Word of God declares that Satan has only come to destroy life and that he was a murderer since the beginning (1 Pet. 5:8; John 8:44). Again, this is only my belief and explanation for the extinction of dinosaurs. What is certain is that God cast Satan to earth. Satan then took the physical form of a serpent to deceive Eve. This means that Satan was on earth before God created man.

God is holy. His holiness is a consuming fire (Heb. 12:29). He is pure. God did not create evil. God did not create sin. There is not one speck of pride or sin in God or in his heavenly kingdom. God created the heart of Lucifer, but God did not create pride.

Lucifer discerned pride just as we all discerned the ways of evil. Lucifer embraced pride and became the father of sin. In other words, pride and sin originated from him. Pride transformed Lucifer into a devil.

Sin is anything outside of God. Sin is a lie and a perversion of God's truth. Jesus said concerning some Pharisees and Satan:

> *You are of your father the devil and the lusts of your father you will do. He was a murderer since the beginning, and abode not in the truth, because there is no truth in him.*

When he speaketh a lie, he speaketh of his own; for he is a liar and the father of it.

—John 8:44

Satan deceives the nations and accuses the saints. Every lie imaginable comes from Satan. Any doubt of God's Word comes from Satan. Any truth that is revealed to you will come from the Holy Spirit.

You can now see how Satan tries to pervert the Word of God in our society. The Word of God says that children are a blessing, but Satan deceives people into believing otherwise. God created matrimony between a man and a woman, but Satan perverts it.

Satan perverts the Word of God through the rebellious heart of man. What type of society would we have if everyone kept the Ten Commandments? It would be heaven on earth.

God created all the different races of the world. He made us all different with different languages. God is the one that gave us our skin color. He made us different to see if our heart is willing to obey his Word rather than our own desires.

God says to love your neighbor as yourself (Matt. 22:39). God sees our hearts and tries our hearts. God sees if there is someone on earth who is willing to walk the way of love and of his Spirit. God is watching from above to see if there is a heart willing to be like him—someone who is willing to even love his enemy. God created different races so that we can learn to love. On the other hand, Satan created racism.

We are not Americans, or Latinos, or Europeans, or Asians, or Africans. We are all spiritual beings made in the image of God. We all came from God, and we all are more spiritual than we think. There is a need in our hearts to have God because our hearts were made for God. Only God can fill us.

Before God created Lucifer, God knew Lucifer would walk into sin and become Satan, which is a perversion of God's will. Before God created the heavens and the earth, God knew that he would cast Satan out of heaven to earth. Why earth? Why didn't God send Satan to a different planet? Because although Satan is evil, Satan still is part of God's perfect plan. God uses Satan as his puppet. Since God cannot tempt men's hearts with evil, he uses Satan.

> *Blessed is the man that endureth temptation: for when he is tried, he shall receive the crown of life, which the Lord hath promised to them that love him. Let no man say when he is tempted, I am tempted of God: for God cannot be tempted with evil, neither tempted he any man: But every man is tempted when he is drawn away of his own lust, and enticed. Then when lust hath conceived, it bringeth forth sin: and sin, when it is finished, bringeth forth death.*
>
> —Jas. 1:12–14

God allows Satan to test men's hearts because God wants to see if we truly love him and trust him. He wants his grace to abound toward us. Our life here on earth is, in essence, a trial of our heart. God will try our hearts to see if we are willing to obey him more than anything else. But be not deceived, we are here to be tried by the Devil because of God's design. We are here to endure and fight every temptation, trial, and tribulation.

Another spiritual law of God is this: if you obey, God will bless you. The blessings and promises of God depend upon our obedience. In order for God to bless us, we must obey. In order for us to choose to obey, we must have the opportunity to disobey. If God did not provide an opportunity for us to disobey then we would be robots and not obedient children.

God made Adam and Eve and blessed them. In order for God to continue to pour out his blessings and glory, they needed to show their obedience to him. Obedience draws the blessings of God. Therefore, God provided an opportunity for them to disobey and planted the Tree of the Knowledge of Good and Evil in the middle of the garden. God then gave them instructions, warnings, and promises. As long as they continued to obey God's Word and not eat of the tree of the Knowledge of Good and Evil, God continued to bless them.

God places us in this world to see if we can bear fruit that is pleasing unto him. If we obey God against all odds, this brings his blessing into our lives. If obedience produces blessing, what does disobedience bring forth? Cursings (read Deuteronomy beginning with chapter 28).

Before God created Adam and Eve, he knew they would sin. Before God created man, the Father knew he would send the Son to shed his blood for our sins. God is holy and where he is, sin cannot abide. If man chooses sin over God, then man must live separated from God in hell. However, through the blood of Jesus Christ, no sin can keep us from God. Sin demands the price of death. Jesus paid that price for us. This is exactly what God wants, that sin should not be able to separate us from him.

Before the foundation of the world, God knew he would choose Israel to impart wisdom and knowledge and hold the Old Testament writings. God knew they would reject Jesus Christ, and salvation would come to the Gentiles. Before the foundation of the world, God knew you. Before the foundation of the world, God knew the beginning and the end time. Before the foundation of the world and before the beginning of time, God predestined the Gentiles to be saved.

When God made the universe, he made time and knew its dispensations. When man began to follow the Spirit, God showed men a window to the future and eternity. All the men of God in the Old and New Testaments were great discerners. God showed Abraham that he would be the father of a multitude. God also showed him that his seed would be in captivity for four-hundred years. God showed him that out of him would come nations and kings and, eventually, the one true seed, Jesus Christ. In the day of Christ, he said, "Abraham rejoiced to see my day; and he saw it and was glad" (John 8:56).

Jesus Christ was angry with the ministers of his day because they could not discern their time. "O ye hypocrites, ye can discern the face of the sky; but can ye not discern the signs of the times" (Matt. 16:3)? Can you discern your time? Jesus Christ said,

Take heed that no man deceive you. For many shall come in my name, saying, I am Christ; and shall deceive many. And ye shall hear of wars and rumours of wars: see that ye

> *be not troubled: for all these things must come to pass, but the end is not yet. For nation shall rise against nation, and kingdom against kingdom: and there shall be famines, and pestilences, and earthquakes, in divers places. All these are the beginning of sorrows. . . . And this gospel of the kingdom shall be preached in all the world for a witness unto all nations; and then shall the end come.*
>
> —Matt. 24:4–8,14

We are in the beginning stage of sorrows moving toward the great and final tribulation. We are moving fast toward the end of time.

What time is it? Jesus said, "Learn the parable of the fig tree; When his branch is yet tender, and putteth forth leaves, ye know that summer is nigh" (Matt. 24:32). The fig tree refers to Israel. "When his branch is tender" might refer to Israel becoming a nation in 1948. "Putting forth leaves" might refer to the prosperity of Israel by the reconstruction of Solomon's Temple. "Summer is nigh" refers to the second coming of Christ.

The Roman army, led by Titus, conquered Jerusalem and destroyed the second temple. The Jewish people were then exiled and scattered. They tried to revolt, but the Romans decimated the Jewish community. The Romans renamed Jerusalem *Aelia Capitolina* and Judea *Palestina* to obliterate Jewish identification with their land. These events took place between 63 A.D. and 313 A.D.

The Jewish homeland was taken over by the heathen. God promised this land specifically to them when he made a covenant with them (Gen. 12:7, 13:14–15, 15:18–21, 17:8). God does not lie. He keeps his covenants.

Jesus prophesied about the destruction of the mighty temple and said that not one stone would be left upon another (Matt. 24:2). This is an accurate prophecy that fulfilled in 70 A.D. when Titus ordered his soldiers to burn the temple down. The Romans took trees from the neighboring countryside to create a giant bonfire. The intense heat caused the moisture in the limestone to expand, and the stones exploded like popcorn, producing a chain reaction of destruction. Today, the magnificent temple is nothing but rubble. (This information was taken from the web site: www.aish.com.)

The Jewish people have been the most scattered people in history because the Jewish people are caught up in a mighty spiritual war. The western world does not understand the conflict between Israel and its Arab neighbors. It is a spiritual war and has nothing to do with reason. I do not intend to go into detail, but I encourage you to read books on the rebuilding of the temple and prophecy.

All I want to impress on your heart right now is that God is in control and has foreseen all of this. The Bible records all of these events. The Dragon is the Devil. The woman who gives birth is Israel. The man-child is Christ. The Dragon is going after the woman in rage (Rev. 12).

God gave time for the Jewish people to come back to their God-given land. God waited about 1,635 years. Then the prophecy went forth. All events—past, present, and future—have been written in his Word. "And he shall set up an ensign for the nations, and shall assemble the outcasts of Israel, and gather together the dispersed of Judah from the four corners of the earth" (Isa. 11:12).

To bring this prophecy to fulfillment, God allowed a satanic force to control hatred toward Jewish people and toward the church. Understand though, God has foreseen it. He turns everything against Satan because God is infinite in wisdom. Satan brought forth his leader, Adolph Hitler (a type of the anti-Christ) to persecute and destroy the Jewish people.

Six million, never again! was a Jewish slogan that inspired the Jews to move to their homeland. By the thousands they came back to the land that God gave them. They submitted to the covenant. Then God miraculously protected them from enemies larger and stronger than they were. God is a jealous God. He knows how to keep his promises.

All the nations around Israel tried to stop them from being a recognized nation, but no one can stop God's people. God promised to be with them always. Why do Israel's neighbors want Israel to give up their promised land? Because Satan wants to pervert the Word of God.

In 1948, the United Nations recognized Israel as a sovereign nation. Keep your eyes on Israel. Israel is the fig tree, an ensign to the nations. There is a spiritual battle raging in God's Holy Land.

Israel and the Palestinians are fighting over a small piece of real estate, the land for the temple mount. To the rest of the world, this battle over the tiny plot is ridiculous. They don't understand that our future is hanging in the outcome.

God predestined the struggle between Israel, Palestine, and the Arabs. It is the struggle between the promised child, Isaac, and his step-brother, Ishmael (Gen. 16:11,12). Both had God's promise that he would become a multitude of people (Gen. 17:20), but the Promised Land was given to the promised child, Isaac. However, they continue to fight for control of their Father Abraham's land.

Israel and the Arabs are fighting over this area because it is a holy site. To the Arabs it is the site of their holy mosque. To the Jewish people, it is the site of their holy temple. The Jewish people desire to control this land, so they can rebuild the temple for the third and final time. Once Israel takes over this land, they will build their temple. They have already prepared everything, from the garments for the priests to the red heifers that will be offered. The Jewish people also claim that they know where the Ark of the Covenant is buried.

Once the Jewish temple is rebuilt, we have a word of prophecy that that generation will not pass away until all things are fulfilled (Matt. 24:32–34). Once the Jewish temple has been rebuild, the final anti-Christ will desecrate the temple (Dan. 9:27). Once the temple is rebuilt, Bible prophecy will come together before your eyes.

The world is being set up for its final stage. Once Israel regains control of the land and has conquered his enemies or has brought peace with his enemies, mankind will enter the final dispensation of God. This final dispensation will bring the construction of the temple, and the world will enter its final tribulation. "For when they shall say, Peace and safety; then sudden destruction cometh upon them, as travail upon a woman with child; and they shall not escape" (1 Thess. 5:3). That's when the world will enter the final book of the Bible, the book of the Revelation.

God's mercy is prolonging that battle in Israel right now. This is the dispensation of grace. God in his mercy and predestination has come to the Gentiles for their salvation. When Israel rejected Jesus Christ, God prophesied that he would go to another people (Hos. 2:23; Rom. 9:25–27). Now is the time of grace. Now is the time when you can cry after God and find him. Soon grace for the Gentiles will be over. God again will focus his attention towards Israel and deal with the remnant until they see the Second Coming of Christ. Then they will confess that Jesus Christ is their Messiah (Isa. 10:22; Rev. 1:7; Phil. 2:11).

God has foreseen everything that is going on in the world. There is nothing Satan has done that has surprised God. God has all wisdom and power. He is in control. He has seen the hearts of man that they love themselves more than God. God has seen the apostasy of the church. God has seen their dependence on politics rather than on the power of God. God has seen men trusting themselves instead of his Word. God has placed a snare on any wisdom that is apart from him.

Nevertheless, God has seen also the latter rain, and the great revival that is going to sweep across this world. When the full number of the Gentiles is complete he will rapture his church. Then all the politicians with their hunger for war and their man-made policies will enter into the great tribulation.

God's power will not move through politics but through his church. God has chosen the weak to confound the strong and the simple to confound the wise. God will unleash his power through the church. It is not the job of politicians to preach salvation and healing but the church. This will be done through God's power and wisdom. What is present is small compared to the wisdom and power that will be unleashed. Our prophets have prophesied, and now our spiritual teachers will teach how to start revival in our hearts. The church is moving into great wisdom and power.

God is in control, not man, nor politicians, nor ministers, nor angels, nor devils. God is in control, not the weather, nor nature. God will bring time to an end, not a nuclear war, nor meteorite, nor any natural catastrophe. The end will take place at his command.

At the end of time, all of humanity will stand before God.

> *And I saw the dead, small and great, stand before God; and the books were opened: and another book was opened, which is the book of life: and the dead were judged out of those things which were written in the books, according to their works. And the sea gave up the dead which were in it; and death and hell delivered up the dead which were in them: and they were judged every man according to their works. And death and hell were cast into the lake of fire. This is the second death. And whosoever was not found written in the book of life was cast into the lake of fire.*
>
> —Rev. 20:11–15

What is written in those books? Every deed, every word, and every thought.

But I say unto you, That every idle word that men shall speak, they shall give account thereof in the day of judgment.

—Matt. 12:36

But I say unto you, that whosoever looketh on a woman to lust after her hath committed adultery with her already in his heart.

—Matt. 5:28

. . . who both will bring to light the hidden things of darkness, and will make manifest the counsels of the hearts: and shall every man have praise of God.

—1 Cor. 4:5

In the day when God shall judge the secrets of men by Jesus Christ according to my gospel.

—Rom. 2:16

Everything that has been done in secret will be known. Every time you spoke evil about someone behind his back, it will be known. Every idle thought that entered your heart will be known. How can anybody escape such a judgment day? This book is dedicated to answering that precise question. There is a way. It is powerful in Christ Jesus.

God is just. He has told us exact events from the past, present, and future. He has hid nothing from us. When the day comes and we stand before him, we won't have any excuse. He has warned us over and over again. The responsibility to prepare for such a day is ours (Matt. 25:1–13, the parable of the ten virgins). To dedicate our lives to preparation for that moment is spiritual wisdom. It transcends all human wisdom.

If God demands high morals from us, don't you think God has also provided the means for us to accomplish his task? If God demands such a high level of obedience, don't you think he also has prepared a way for us to accomplish it? "There hath no temptation taken you but such as is common to man: but God is faithful, who will not suffer you to be tempted above that ye are able; but will with the temptation also make a way to escape, that ye may be able to bear it" (1 Cor. 10:13).

Now you know exactly what is going to happen. The next question your heart should ask is how to escape the coming doom. What is your place in God's perfect plan? What was God's purpose for creating man?

Man's main purpose is to seek God. Make no mistake. Our job here on earth is to seek God. God expects us to set some time aside and seek him. We spend countless hours watching television, making money, or seeking our hobbies, but we fail to answer one question that our eternity hinges on, "Why are we here?"

The only one who can identify the meaning of life is the church. They have the Bible and teach from it. The Word of God has all the answers. However, I do admit, the Bible is written in a spiritual code. Without access to this code there is no harmony. To access its profound teachings you first need to know the author and teacher of the Word of God, the Holy Spirit.

Jesus' first recorded words in the gospel of John were, "What seek ye?" It is incredible how people spend their entire lives seeking everything except God. Everything outside of God is only temporal, yet people die for temporal things.

God became flesh and said he was the light of the world. He came to enlighten us. I hang on every word that he said. "But seek ye first the kingdom of God and his righteousness; and all these things shall be added unto you" (Matt. 6:33). ". . . seek and ye shall find" (Matt. 7:7).

Without a doubt, God has placed the sole responsibility on us to seek him. Do not wait for God to seek you. God did not lose you, he knows exactly where you are. He sees you reading this book. You need to seek God because you are the one that is lost.

> *This is the generation of them that seek him, that seek thy face, O Jacob.*
>
> —Ps. 24:6

> *One thing have I desired of the Lord, that will I seek after; that I may dwell in the house of the Lord all the days of my life, to behold the beauty of the Lord, and to inquire in his temple. For in the time of trouble he shall hide me in his pavilion: in the secret of his tabernacle shall he hide me; he shall set me up upon a rock.*

> *And now shall mine head be lifted up above mine enemies round about me: therefore will I offer in his tabernacle sacrifices of joy; I will sing, yea, I will sing praises unto the Lord. Hear, O Lord, when I cry with my voice: have mercy also upon me, and answer me.*

> *When thou saidst, Seek ye my face; my heart said unto thee, Thy face, Lord, will I seek. Hide not thy face far from me; put not thy servant away in anger: thou hast been my help; leave me not, neither forsake me, O God of my salvation.*
>
> —Ps. 27:4–9

> *Seek ye the Lord, all ye meek of the earth, which have wrought his judgment; seek righteousness, seek meekness: it may be ye shall be hid in the day of the Lord's anger.*
>
> —Zeph. 2:3

The best advice King David gave his son, Solomon is the best advice our heavenly father gives us.

> *My son, know thou the God of thy father, and serve him with a perfect heart and with a willing mind: for the Lord searcheth all hearts, and understandeth all the imaginations of the thoughts: if thou seek him he will be found of thee; but if thou forsake him, he will cast thee off for ever.*
>
> —1 Chron. 28:9

God promises that if you seek him diligently, you will find him. Anyone who wants to know more of God will find more and more knowledge. If you do not want to know God, you have to do a good job of hiding your head in the ground. "I love them that love me; and those that seek me early shall find me" (Prov. 8:17). "And ye shall seek me, and find me, when ye shall search for me with all your heart" (Jer. 29:13).

Why don't people seek God?

> *The Lord looked down from heaven upon the children of men, to see if there were any that did understand, and seek God. They are all gone aside, they are all together become filthy: there is none that doeth good, no, not one.*
>
> —Ps. 14:2–3

> *The wicked through the pride of his countenance, will not seek after God: God is not in all his thoughts.*
>
> —Ps. 10:4

When men die, they will stand before Jesus Christ, and he will ask them, "Why didn't you seek me when you had the time?" Have you prepared an answer when your time comes?

> *Seek ye the Lord while he may be found, call ye upon him while he is near.*
>
> —Isa. 55:6

Chapter 4

WALKING IN GOD'S PERFECT WILL

That the ages to come he may show the exceeding riches of his grace in his kindness towards us through Christ Jesus. . . . For we are his workmanship, created in Christ Jesus unto good works, which God has before ordained that we should walk in them.

—Eph. 2:7,10

We know in theory that God is all powerful and all knowing. However, God doesn't want us to live in theory. He wants us to live in the reality of his power and wisdom. God does not want us to act *as if* we know him; he wants us to *really know* him. A lack of revelation knowledge keeps us from God. If we reject knowledge, than God will reject us also (Hos. 4:6).

If God knows all things and sees all things and if he has predestined all things, what can we do? How do we fit into God's perfect plan? It is so simple and yet so brilliant that we miss it.

Listen to me, if God has put everything into motion, if God has all power and wisdom, then the only thing we can do is simply ***submit***. Here before you is revelation knowledge. Submit to the Word of God and to the Spirit of God.

Take a moment and meditate on what you just read.

God is the only one who can orchestrate our future. If we submit to God, he will bring harmony and order into our lives. He brings harmony to everything he touches. You have the ability to make choices. Once you choose to obey, you have chosen God's will for your life.

God has predestined a beautiful life for you. The moment you choose to obey God above yourself, you are telling God that you trust him with your life. This act of faith produces obedience and declares that you have reached a mature spiritual level. You trust God more than you trust yourself. Trusting God's wisdom rather than your own wisdom produces a very different or **peculiar** way of life (Deut. 14:2; Tit. 2:14; I Pet. 2:9).

The moment you choose to obey God, he begins to unfold his perfect plan for your life. The moment you obey God, you begin to rely on a higher wisdom. The moment you choose to submit to God, your life shifts to a custom-made path that is blessed and ordained of God. Do you see how important it is to obey God? The following chapters will teach you exactly *how* and *why* to obey God.

In God's predestined lifestyle, whatever comes into your life is by divine appointment. You will know that you are a person of destiny. You will be in awe. Destiny is upon you.

The moment you completely trust God, you take your first steps on water. You begin exploring God's perfect will for your life.

Before, we made the mistake of trusting our abilities, our strength, our power, our resources, and our wisdom. We limited the power of God in our lives. This makes perfect sense. If we do anything by ourselves, we get the glory. If we do things by God's grace, God receives the glory. God has proclaimed in his Word that he does not share his glory with anyone.

God does not do anyone's bidding if it does not line up with his will. Obedience to his Word is his will. God is very sensitive when it comes to sharing the spotlight. Lucifer discovered this spiritual truth when he was kicked out of heaven. It is all of him and none of us. "I am the Lord: that is my name: and my glory will I not give to another . . ." (Isa. 42:8).

It is impossible for God to contradict his Word because he is not a man that he should lie. We cannot approach God's throne and ask God to contradict his Word. It has not happened since the beginning of man. It will not happen today, or tomorrow.

We ask God to answer our prayers to satisfy our own egos. We ask God to use us for our own will, purpose, and agenda. We need to approach God's throne and ask him for revelation knowledge to know his ways. We need to ask for wisdom because in its left hand is life and in its right hand is honor and riches (Prov. 3:13–16).

God will not use our flesh, our abilities, or anything that will bring glory to us. God will not use our man-made titles. God will not use our knowledge of books that gives us confidence in ourselves. Our confidence should be in him. God does not need our wisdom. He proclaims:

> *For you see your calling, brethren, how that not many wise men after the flesh, not many mighty, not many noble, are called: but God hath chosen the foolish things of the world to confound the wise; and God hath chosen the weak things of the world to confound the things which are mighty; and base things of the world, and things which are not, to bring to nought things that are. That no flesh should glory in his presence.*
>
> —1 Cor. 1:26–29

When Paul understood that God did not need his wisdom but his yielded heart, Paul proclaimed:

> *But what things were gain to me, those I counted loss for Christ. Yea doubtless, and I count all things but loss for the excellency of the knowledge of Christ Jesus my Lord: for whom I have suffered the loss of all things, and do count them but dung, that I may win Christ, and be found in him, not having mine own righteousness, which is of the law, but that which is through the faith of Christ, the righteousness which is of God by faith: That I may know him and the power of his resurrection, and the fellowship of his sufferings, being made conformable unto his death.*
>
> —Phil. 3:7–10

What type of vessel is God going to use to usher in the latter rain? Yielded vessels. These are the ministers that God has chosen. They are not doctors. They do not have any

PhDs or pride themselves in being called *Reverend*. Their only title is, "Prisoner and Servant of Christ Jesus!"

These grace ministers may not have much training. Their achievements may seem small in the natural sense, but in the supernatural they have years of training. They are mighty in the Spirit. They do not possess head knowledge but heart knowledge. They do not possess a doctrinal mind but a heart full of love and compassion. Their loyalty is not to denominations or to men but to the Word of God and his Spirit. They do not depend on men but solely on God's grace. They are not led by their souls. They are led by the Spirit.

God is calling us to depend on him, a still higher level of faith. God has called us to enter into his rest— total relief from our works and total dependence on him.

> *There remaineth therefore a rest to the people of God. For he that is entered into his rest, he also hath ceased from his own works, as God did from his. Let us labour therefore to enter into that rest, lest any man fall after the same example of unbelief.*
>
> —Heb. 4:9–11

Once we understand how to labour into this rest God has prepared for us, God will move in our behalf. When we learn to rest from our works and depend on God, then the Holy Spirit will once again move among his church as he did in the book of Acts.

What would you do to receive power from God to have victory over your fleshly passions? What would you do to have the glory, power, and wisdom of God flowing through you to reach this blind and dying world? What would you do to experience the supernatural in your life? What would you do to experience the reality of your Creator? Would you submit to God and allow God to work his power in you?

God has everything figured out. It is up to us to understand his truth and enter into his plan. For an example of God's all-knowing wisdom and power: we can do nothing to earn salvation. It is impossible. We can never be worthy of such a great salvation. God preordained everything, even the bloody death of his Son as our substitute. We depend not on our works but on the works of Jesus Christ. We accept his works on the cross by faith and receive God's grace for salvation. This is all God's doing. All we are required to do is submit, accept it, and grow in it.

Everything is done through God's grace. Everything God gives us is not because of our works but because of God's works. This is why he receives all the glory. We simply accept his works by faith that it may truly be a gift of God. Every calling, anointing, ministry—we receive them through faith that it may be of grace. "And if by grace then it is no more by works: otherwise grace is no more grace. But if it be of works, then is it no more grace: otherwise work is no more work" (Rom. 11:6).

We live in the dispensation of God's grace. The time of grace will not last forever. We now have a short time to understand and grow in grace in order to accomplish God's will on earth. God's purpose and glory will flow through us, but we will not control it. After God works through us we will stand back and proclaim, "This is the Lord's doing; it is marvelous in our eyes" (Ps. 118:23).

The whole world exists because of God's grace. If it wasn't for God's grace, he would have destroyed all of humanity back in Genesis chapter six, but Noah found grace in the eyes of the Lord.

> *And God saw that the wickedness of man was great in the earth, and that every imagination of the thoughts of his heart was only evil continually. And it repented the Lord that he had made man on the earth, and it grieved him at his heart. And the Lord said, I will destroy man whom I have created from the face of the earth. . . . But Noah found grace in the eyes of the Lord.*
>
> —Gen. 6:5–8

The earth is inhabited today because of the few who found grace in the eyes of God. We exist and depend on God without realizing it. We exist because the mercy of God makes the sun rise every morning upon the just and unjust. We depend on the rain that God showers on us. We exist because we breathe God's air. We awake every morning because God put order and strength into our human body. From birth, we depend on the wisdom and harmony that God has placed in the physical realm.

If God's wisdom knows how much to tilt the earth to make our seasons, if he set the earth a comfortable distance from the sun, can't we place our lives in his hands? If God's wisdom made the human body to breathe on its own, pump blood on its own, and heal on its own, can't we trust God with our lives? If God put prophecy in his Bible and we see its fulfillment, can't we trust God with our lives? If God brought harmony to the plant and animal kingdoms so they can exist on their own, can't we depend on God? If God provides shelter and food for the birds, aren't we more important to him than birds?

It is by grace, so no man or no flesh can boast. "Where is boasting then? It is excluded. By what law? Of works? Nay: but by the law of faith" (Rom. 3:27). "For by grace are you saved through faith; and that not of yourselves: it is the gift of God: Not of works, lest any man should boast" (Eph. 2:8,9).

God will not share his glory with man. Man has been predestined to submit to God so that God's glory can flow through man. God receives all the glory because this is all his doing. If we submit to him, God will take us on the ride of our lives.

Without God's grace upon us we can do nothing. We cannot please him; we cannot minister effectively; we cannot conquer our fleshly desires. We cannot produce fruit that is pleasing to him, let alone enter his throne in prayer.

Jesus said,

> *Abide in me and I in you. As the branch cannot bear fruit of itself, except it abide in the vine; no more can ye except ye abide in me. I am the vine ye are the branches: He that abideth in me and I in him, the same bringeth forth much fruit: for without me ye can do nothing.*
>
> —John 15:4–5

Grace is a key factor in accomplishing the will of God. It is the key to understanding your purpose on earth. The men of the Old Testament labored to find grace in the eyes of God. Time after time they begged God and said, "Let me find grace in thy sight," or, ". . . if I found grace in thy sight." The challenge is now before us to grow in God's grace.

Faith initiates the process of receiving God's grace but humility intensifies it. God gives more grace to the humble (Jas. 4:6). This is the secret to receiving more grace from God. Yet, it is an open secret because it has been proclaimed since the beginning of man. The only thing that has stopped the church from understanding this truth is revelation knowledge. To achieve this knowledge we must understand all the dynamics involved and why one must have a humble attitude.

A person with a humble heart understands that everything happens because God is in control, and, therefore, he submits to God.

The words *humility*, *submit*, *yield*, *meekness*, and *obedience* make the flesh cringe because in the flesh is the law of sin. Demons cringe at the word *submission* because they can't submit. All they know is pride and rebellion. They are damned beings that influence and captivate the minds of millions.

These words of submission seem weak in the natural realm, but in the spiritual realm they are mighty to the pulling down of strongholds. This is the secret place where God wants us to be, in complete submission to the Holy Spirit. Once you submit, God's power comes into your life and frees you. As your submission grows, God's hand moves more mightily upon you. There is no limit to God's power in our lives except the limit set by our pride.

If you permit Satan to deceive you into believing that submission is weak, you will be held captive at that level of understanding. The Holy Spirit can show you the opposite is true. It is written that even the weak things of God are stronger than the things of men (1 Cor. 1:25). Submission to Jesus Christ is liberty, wisdom, power, and communion with the Holy Spirit. There is nothing in us that God desires or needs. Nothing pleases him except our willingness to submit to him by obeying his Word.

In the Old Testament, time after time when an individual or nation humbled themselves, God always forgave them no matter how great their sin was. There is something about a humble heart that is irresistible to God. The moment a person humbles his heart, God begins to deal with the individual. A humble heart is precious to God.

> *But let it be the hidden man of the heart, in that which is not corruptible, even the ornament of a meek and quiet spirit which is in the sight of God of great price.*
>
> —1 Pet. 3:4

Listen carefully. God adores a humble attitude. The psalmist David understood that a humble and contrite heart, God will not despise (Ps. 51:17). God himself proclaims, "For thus saith the high and lofty One that inhabiteth eternity, whose name is holy; I dwell in the high and holy place, with him also that is of contrite and humble spirit, to revive the spirit of the humble and to revive the heart of the contrite ones" (Isa. 57:15).

God dwells in a humble heart. God does not dwell in emotion or good works, which are only a natural result when the Creator touches your heart. God does not dwell in your mind. You will find God only when you humble yourself and ask for his grace to obey. God is only found in a contrite heart.

It is no coincidence that Moses was the meekest man on earth. Moses was the one to behold the glory of God (Num. 12:3). A meek heart and God's glory go hand in hand. Only a meek heart can remain in meekness after being touched by the glory of God.

When God's grace is upon your life, everything you do will be blessed. God will bless your finances. God will bless your marriage. God will bless you mentally, emotionally, and physically. God's grace issues the power of God into your life.

"Humble yourselves under the mighty hand of God that in due time he may exalt you." If you let these words of submission be a stumbling block for you then you will never experience the mighty hand of God in your life. You're doomed to have mere religion. You will always be learning and never attaining the truth (2 Tim. 3:7).

Without submission, you will only have a form of godliness but denying the power thereof with your words and actions (2 Tim. 3:5). As Christians, all we have to do is submit. God will do the rest. That is the greatest deal anyone can offer. This is the greatest deal anyone can offer you.

How exactly do we accomplish this spiritual task of submission to God's Word? **We have to submit all imaginations, all thoughts, all desires, all emotions, all feelings, all opinions, all criticism—everything that is within us—and bring them into obedience to Jesus Christ.** I call this submitting our inward being to God.

The process of submitting the inward being to God is what the Holy Spirit has wanted for his people since time began. This is the central task of all humans. God wanted this in both the Old and New Testaments. God wanted this for both Israel and the Christian church. Both were instructed to love the Lord thy God with all their heart, all their soul, and with all their strength (Deut. 10:12; Luke 10:27). This is God's plan for us so that we may live with a higher power in our lives.

The New Testament refers to submission to God over and over again.

> *For he is not a Jew, which is one outwardly; neither is that circumcision, which is outward in the flesh: but he is a Jew, which is one inwardly; and circumcision is that of the heart, in the spirit, and not in the letter; whose praise is not of men, but of God.*
>
> —Rom. 2:28–29

Submission begins the process of renewing our mind (Rom. 12:2). This is symbolized through water baptism. Jesus Christ refers to submission as carrying your cross and denying yourself (Matt. 16:24; Mark 8:34; Luke 9:23). This process is also known as dying to self.

We accomplish submission with our faith and, eventually, by the grace of God. In other words, as we take the first steps of faith, God's sees our faith and sends us grace so we can submit still more. When we start believing that God is able to do what he says, God sees our faith and strengthens us with his might.

God is vitally concerned with our inward being (our heart). He knows that we speak and act from our inward being (Matt. 12:24–35). What goes on in our inward beings either pleases or displeases God (Rom. 2:29). Therefore, our number-one focus should be our inward beings. "Behold, thou desirest truth in the inward parts: and in the hidden part thou shalt make me to know wisdom" (Ps. 51:6).

Every time you deny yourself for the sake of the gospel, the Creator is pleased. Joy and peace fills your heart as he draws closer to you. This is what Christians should strive to attain. The church has a responsibility to teach new converts how to dwell in the presence of God. Without God's presence, Christianity is only another dry religion of do's and don'ts.

The process of dying to self represents only the beginning of the Christian life. When you die to self, you open a spiritual door so that God comes into your life with his grace and wisdom.

The presence of God will bring harmony to your life. The presence of God will fill your heart and give you a reason to live. I cannot emphasize enough the importance of the presence of God is in our lives. God designed your heart for his presence.

Your heart was made by God and for God to bear much fruit. Your heart was designed to function with faith, hope, and love. You carry within you such understanding of spiritual things.

For example, when someone treats you wrongly and you react with indifference, you have hardened your heart. The presence of God is far from you and bitterness reigns in your life. On the other hand, if someone offends you and you decide to treat him well anyway, then the presence of God has worked in your life. Soon, you will learn to avoid those things that leave you empty and bitter. You will grow in things that fill your life with love, joy, and peace in the Holy Spirit (Rom. 14:17).

The Holy Spirit is truth. Through our conscience, he guides us into the correct path where we can find God. He guides us to a life of brokenness where he abides. The cross, which Jesus spoke about, symbolizes the attitude of a broken heart and a contrite spirit. Whoever has spiritual ears let him receive revelation knowledge of spiritual truths.

All the New Testament teachings refer to his presence by referring to the Spirit. Without the teachings of the Spirit, religion is simply man trying to please God with his deeds, his logic, and his traditions. When men study the Word of God, they are instructed to focus not on the letter but on the Spirit in which the letter was written.

God will never be found in the letter. Religion is found in the letter. "Who also hath made us able ministers of the New Testament; not of the letter, but of the spirit: for the letter killeth, but the spirit giveth life" (2 Cor. 3:6). The result of submitting your inward being to Christ is, ". . . that we should serve in newness of the Spirit, and not in the oldness of the letter" (Rom. 7:6).

Let me reiterate this one point: The Word of God deals primarily with spiritual principles that produce virtues or fruit. Spiritual principles deal with the presence of God in our hearts. Without the spiritual side of the Bible, we have no Bible. Without the Spirit we can do nothing. Because of the Spirit we can obey God's Word. The grace of God gives us the Holy Spirit so we can completely submit to God. "That he would grant you according to the riches of his glory, to be strengthened with might by his Spirit in the inner man" (Eph. 3:16).

How do you die to self? Obedience to God's Word brings death to self. How can we obey completely? By submitting to Jesus Christ our inward being, one thought at a time.

> *Casting down imaginations and every high thing that exalteth itself against the knowledge of God, and bringing into captivity every thought to the obedience of Christ.*
>
> —2 Cor. 10:5

There it is! Bring every thought captive to the obedience of Jesus Christ! Let our five-fold ministers shout it from the rooftops! Wake up and pay attention!

There are only two lifestyles: one that pleases God and one that pleases self. One leads to heaven to be with God, the other leads to hell (separation from God). God has already predestined the results of these two lifestyles. The Bible describes their fruits of the Spirit, or works of the flesh. The only thing God can do is show you the truth. You alone will decide the path you take.

When you bring every thought to the obedience of Jesus Christ, God renews your mind. In the process, God will deal with you about life's meaning. God will reveal his perfect will for you. "And be not conformed to this world: but be ye transformed by the renewing of your mind, that ye may prove what is that good, and acceptable, and perfect, will of God" (Rom. 12:2).

If you do not bring every thought to the obedience of Jesus Christ, you will develop a reprobate mind. The following passage shows what happens when a person does not bring every thought captive to Jesus Christ:

> *And even as they did not like to retain God in their knowledge, God gave them over to a reprobate mind, to do those things which are not convenient; being filled with all unrighteousness, fornication, wickedness, covetousness, maliciousness; full of envy, murder, debate, deceit, malignity; whisperers, backbiters, haters of God, despiteful, proud, boasters, inventors of evil things, disobedient to parents, without understanding, covenant breakers, without natural affection, implacable, unmerciful: who knowing the judgment of God, that they which commit such things are worthy of death, not only do the same, but have pleasure in them that do them.*
>
> —Rom. 1:24–32

If you refuse to set your mind to seeking God, you are predestined to have a cursed and tormented mind (Deut. 28:28; 2 Tim. 1:7). *Renewing your mind with the word of God was never an option for mankind. It is the duty of mankind.*

What mind do you have: a reprobate mind or a renewed mind? Can you see the benefit, the wisdom, and power of having a renewed mind?

When you submit your inward being to God you are also submitting your soul to him. Your soul holds your thoughts which regulate your emotions and will. Submitting to Jesus Christ will save your soul. Once you start this process, do not give up. Continue to the end. "But we are not of them who draw back unto perdition; but of them that believe to the saving of the soul" (Heb. 10:39). If you continue in this process then you will experience what the Bible refers to as the prospering of your soul. ". . . even as thy soul prospereth" (3 John 1:2).

You preserve your soul blameless by the grace of God giving you power to submit your inmost being to God.

> *. . . and I pray God your whole spirit and soul and body be preserved blameless unto the coming of our Lord Jesus Christ.*
>
> —1 Thess. 5:23

> *Receive with meekness the engrafted word, which is able to save your souls.*
>
> —Jas. 1:21

> *Seeing ye have purified your souls in obeying the truth through the Spirit . . .*
>
> —1 Pet. 1:22

Submission gives us revelation knowledge to understand what the Bible means when it refers to being "in Christ Jesus." Being in Christ Jesus means being in the Word. Therefore, if we submit and obey God's Word, then we are in Christ. It is no longer I that live but Christ Jesus in me. "I am crucified with Christ: nevertheless I live; yet not I, but Christ liveth in me: and the life which I now live in the flesh I live by the faith of the Son of God, who loved me, and gave himself for me" (Gal. 2:20).

God has predestined a wonderful place where the church can take refuge. David the psalmist knew this place. He called it the secret place (Ps. 91:1). This secret place is in Jesus Christ, ". . . who has blessed us with all spiritual blessings in heavenly places in Christ . . ." (Eph. 1:3).

The whole process of submitting our entire soul to Christ allows us to be reconciled to God. When we submit, we become a new creature in Christ.

> *For in Christ Jesus neither circumcision availed anything, nor uncircumcision, but a new creature.*
>
> —Gal. 6:15

> *Therefore if any man be in Christ, he is a new creature: old things are passed away; behold, all things are become new . . . that God was in Christ, reconciling the world unto himself, not imputing their trespasses unto them; and hath committed unto us the word of reconciliation. Now then we are ambassadors for Christ, as though God did beseech you by us: we pray you in Christ's stead, be ye reconciled to God. For he hath made him to be sin for us, who knew no sin; that we might be made the righteousness of God in him.*
>
> —2 Cor. 5:17

Now, we can be in Christ Jesus and become a new creature. Now, we can lay hold of all the promises that pertain to being "in Christ Jesus." This is the perfect will of God for our lives: to submit our souls to Christ Jesus that we may be in Christ Jesus. "There is neither Jew nor Greek, there is neither bond nor free, there is neither male nor female: for ye are all one in Christ Jesus" (Gal. 3:28).

As you begin the process of submitting your soul to Christ, you will realize that the grace of God has come into your life. For once you were in bondage to sin and desire. Now by the grace of God you are free. Jesus Christ gives you the power to bring your thoughts to obedience. Only God can do this. It will be marvelous in your eyes.

What brought you into bondage before now has no power over you. It cannot bring you into bondage again because Jesus has set you free. All you did was submit, submit, and submit again, and the power of God came into you.

Men seek many means to relieve their emotional and mental ailments, but the word of psychologists or any other men do not hold power like the Word of God. God's sole interest is to help you. He knows you, and loves you, and has even given his life for you. It is up to you to take advantage of this abundant grace that is provided for you.

In our own abilities there is no answer for the world today.

> *For I know that in me (that is, in my flesh,) dwelleth no good thing: for to will is present with me; but how to perform that which is good I find not. For the good that I would I do not: but the evil which I would not, that I do. Now if I do that I would not, it is no more I that do it, but sin that dwelleth in me. I find then a law, that, when I would do good, evil is present with me.*
>
> —Rom. 7:18–21

However, in Jesus Christ you will find the answer to all your needs. If you need deliverance, it is in Jesus Christ. If you need love, it is in Jesus Christ. If you need wisdom, it is in Jesus Christ. If you need your void filled, it is in Jesus Christ.

Therefore, you bring every thought captive to the obedience of Christ that your thoughts and life may be in Christ.

> *For I delight in the law of God after the inward man: But I see another law in my members, warring against the law of my mind, and bringing me into captivity to the law of sin which is in my members. O wretched man that I am! Who shall deliver me from the body of this death? I thank God through Jesus Christ our Lord. . . . There is therefore now no condemnation to them which are in Christ Jesus, who walk not after the flesh but after the Spirit.*
>
> —Rom. 7:22–8:1

You cannot conquer sin on your own. Your mental abilities cannot conquer sin, no matter how intelligent you are. Your will cannot conquer sin, no matter how strong you are. Your dedication to God cannot conquer sin, no matter how much you read the Bible, how much you pray, or how much you give to God. If you say that you can conquer sin by your own power that is a lie, because only the law of sin abides in our flesh (1 John 1:8).

No one can conquer sin in his own human strength no matter who they are. It doesn't matter what position or title—if they are presidents, if they have the most brilliant minds in the world, if they have all the gold in the world, if they are the most anointed preachers of our day, or have the greatest faith. Everyone needs Jesus Christ and the grace he bestows on us. We all need to bring our thoughts before the Lord.

Many ministers, including myself, study the Word of God and preach wonderful anointed sermons, yet, we realize that evil is still present in our flesh. This is the law of sin and death that abides in our flesh (Rom. 7:21).

Here is how to defeat sin in your life: you must submit your soul to Jesus Christ. When you persistently continue to submit, sin loses power over you. Soon you will realize that a greater power has come into you. It is the resurrected power of the Holy Spirit. You are no longer under the law of sin but under the law of grace (Rom. 6:14).

Only by the grace of God can you conquer sin. Great grace comes upon you through a humble heart. Your Creator provided grace for you to bring everything that is inside of you to his feet. All you have to do is continue to submit. God will do the rest. What you could not do on your own, by the resurrection power of Jesus Christ you can now do through grace. "For the law of the Spirit of life in Christ Jesus hath made me free from the law of sin and death" (Rom. 8:2).

Do not live in opinions, in offenses, in criticisms, in the soul but live in the Spirit (complete obedience to the Word of God). There is no excuse because through Jesus Christ, grace is available to everyone in great abundance. There is no shortage of grace just as there is no shortage of power in God.

When we submit all our soul to him, we die to our will. Our submission increases as the Holy Spirit enlightens us about the depth, the length, the breadth, and the height of this spiritual truth. If we are dead to ourselves, we become like Jesus Christ in his death. If we do what he did (die) then the Holy Spirit that raised Jesus from the dead will also quicken our mortal bodies to live in newness of life (Eph. 2:1–5).

> *Therefore we are buried with him by baptism into death: that like as Christ was raised up from the dead by the glory of the Father, even so we also should walk in newness of life.*

For if we have been planted together in the likeness of his death, we shall be also in the likeness of his resurrection: Knowing this, that our old man is crucified with him, that the body of sin might be destroyed, that henceforth we should not serve sin. For he that is dead is freed from sin.

Now if we be dead with Christ, we believe that we shall also live with him: Knowing that Christ being raised from the dead dieth no more; death hath no more dominion over him. For in that he died, he died unto sin once: but in that he liveth, he liveth unto God.

—Rom. 6:4–10

Water baptism is a physical act that symbolizes a spiritual occurrence in the Christian's life. Water baptism symbolizes the truth of dying to self and arising to a new life in Christ Jesus.

Likewise reckon ye also yourselves to be dead indeed unto sin, but alive unto God through Jesus Christ our Lord. Let not sin therefore reign in your mortal body, that ye should obey it in the lusts thereof.

Neither yield ye your members as instruments of unrighteousness unto sin: but yield yourselves unto God, as those that are alive from the dead, and your members as instruments of righteousness unto God. For sin shall not have dominion over you: for ye are not under the law, but under grace.

—Rom. 6:11–14

This concept is vital for us to practice these teachings and to teach them to others. We submit our soul to Jesus

Christ, a process called *death to self*. Death to self is only the beginning. We are buried in death that we may arise to new life in Jesus Christ and bring much fruit. Jesus said,

> *Verily, verily, I say unto you, Except a corn of wheat fall into the ground and die, it abideth alone: but if it die, it bringeth forth much fruit. He that loveth his life shall lose it; and he that hateth his life in this world shall keep it unto life eternal.*
>
> —John 12:24–25

> *Thou fool, that which thou sowest is not quickened, except it die.*
>
> —1 Cor. 15:36

> *So is the kingdom of God, as if a man should cast seed into the ground; and should sleep, and rise night and day, and the seed should spring and grow up, he knoweth not how. For the earth bringeth forth fruit of herself; first the blade, then the ear, after that the full corn in the ear. But when the fruit is brought forth, immediately he putteth in the sickle, because the harvest is come.*
>
> —Mark 4:26–29

We are the seed in this parable. We are buried in death. At first, all we can see is the infant blade springing up from the soil. We know we are different, that power has come into our lives. Sometimes we do not even know that we have changed until someone points it out to us. Finally, we produce fruit that pleases God.

People who have not submitted their souls to God cannot produce fruit because they are slaves to sin. How can someone with emotional problems love their neighbors when all they want to do is kill their enemy? They need to submit their emotions to God. They need to die to their emotions so the power of the Spirit may be upon them. They need to die to self in order to please God and produce the fruit of Spirit that is pleasing unto God . . . one thought at a time.

Once you recognize that it is the power of God in you that keeps your mind from the bondage of sin you will understand clearly what the Word of God is trying to say. Once you understand that it is the power of the spirit within you, everything will make sense. It is all because of the power of Jesus Christ. Paul understood this power. He did everything through the grace of God and not through his own abilities. The apostles did not have any confidence in the flesh. They put their confidence in the power of God (Phil. 3:3).

> *Jesus said, "It is the spirit that quickeneth; the flesh profiteth nothing: the words that I speak unto you, they are spirit, and they are life.*
>
> —John 6:63

> *So then they that are in the flesh cannot please God. But ye are not in the flesh, but in the Spirit, if so be that the Spirit of God dwell in you. Now if any man have not the Spirit of Christ, he is none of his.*
>
> *And if Christ be in you, the body is dead because of sin; but the Spirit is life because of righteousness. But if the Spirit of him that raised up Jesus from the dead dwell in you, he that raised up Christ from the dead shall also quicken your mortal bodies by his Spirit that dwelleth in you.*
>
> —Rom. 8:8–11

We need more revelation knowledge of the word *quicken* in order to understand its profound significance. It is easy to gloss over the word *quicken* and not grasp its power. The spirit will quicken our mortal bodies. We do not quicken ourselves. We have tried and tried and tried and tried to please God by ourselves, by our power, our will, our emotions, our sacrifices, our devotion, our commitment, our intelligence, our desire to please God—only to fail miserably. We cannot please God because he sees all of that as flesh. The only way we can please God is by submitting our soul to Christ.

Meditate on that for a moment. Who is going to quicken your mortal body? God. It is not you. You are not going to take any glory. You cannot declare that you conquered your thoughts by your mighty willpower. No! No! No! Your willpower does not have enough power to quicken your body.

> *And you hath he quickened, who were dead in trespasses and sins: Wherein time past ye walked according to the course of this world, according to the prince of the power of the air, the spirit that now worketh in the children of disobedience: Among whom also we all had our conversation in times past in the lusts of the flesh, fulfilling the desires of the flesh and of the mind; and were by nature the children of wrath, even as others. But God who is rich in mercy, for his great love wherewith he loved us, even when we were dead in sins, hath quicken us together in Christ.*
>
> —Eph. 2:1–5

As I look back on my life, I was full of seducing devils, full of rebellion, full of criticism, full of hate, full of envy, and just full of myself. I am now full of gratitude to God for bringing me out of that miry mud and putting my feet on a rock. Only God has done this. Only God could do this. I serve an awesome God. I feel so humble at the presence of a wonderful, mighty God. Now, my cup runneth over with joy, peace, and love. God will do this for all those who submit to him.

My brother, begin to submit to God and grow in grace so the Spirit of great power may be upon you. We do not control nor manipulate this power. We are simply led by the Spirit.

> *Now we have received, not the spirit of the world, but the spirit which is of God; that we might know the things that are freely given to us of God.*
>
> —1 Cor. 2:12

> *For God has not given us the spirit of fear; but of power, and of love, and of a sound mind.*
>
> —2 Tim. 1:7

Many Christians have an identity crisis because they do not fully understand this chapter. They are stuck between two worlds: the world of the Spirit and the world of the flesh. Once this teaching is proclaimed, then they will understand how to bring their soul into submission to the Spirit and become a new species in Christ. They will be a new creation, born of the Word of God, which is water and Spirit (John 3:3–6).

> *Seeing ye have purified your souls in obeying the truth through the Spirit unto unfeigned love of the brethren, see that ye love one another with a pure heart fervently: Being born again, not of corruptible seed, but of incorruptible, by the word of God, which liveth and abideth for ever.*
>
> —1 Pet. 1:22,23

Right now, you can bring an end to the spiritual war within you and become a new creature in Christ. Give your inward being to Christ. Yield your soul to the obedience of the word of God. Yield your thoughts, desires, emotions, feelings, criticisms, and opinions. Submit all of your being, all your spiritual world within you until it is not you but the reflection of Jesus in your heart. He will bring harmony to your spiritual universe as he did to the physical universe.

Soon you will realize that the resurrection power has come into your life and has defeated sin in you. You no longer give in to the flesh, but now you follow the Spirit. You no longer pursue things that make you empty. You now seek things that fill you with meaning. You will realize that there is no grace, anointing, power, or wisdom in sin, instead only emptiness.

Soon the Holy Spirit will fill the emptiness in your heart. Where there was no love for anyone, you will have a cup full. You will not need love from your spouse or anyone else because your cup is full and running over. Instead of demanding love, you will give love. Where fear and worry dominated your life, now Christ Jesus will fill you with peace and joy. When you come to church, you will worship God with hands lifted and tears streaming down your cheeks because God has done this in your life, and it is marvelous. All you did was submit to him. He did everything for you. Glory be to God forever!

When the five-fold ministries concentrate on the resurrection power, revival will come into the land. This is our destiny. Jesus Christ is the first to resurrect, and we are to follow. We are called to live with resurrection power in these earthen vessels. Our new life in Christ is a resurrected life. "That I may know him and the power of the resurrection . . ." (Phil. 3:10)

Once you have tasted the power of God it is impossible to go back to the flesh (Heb. 6). Once we walk with grace, will we go back to bondage? Never! There is nothing in the flesh but fear and emptiness. Press forward into this new life of faith, hope, and love. As you continue to trust in that grace and seek God's Spirit in all things, you will understand that you have begun to walk on water. A different law is at work in you, the law of the Spirit and of grace.

If you humble yourself and submit your soul to God, you will hold the world in the palm of your hand. The earth and everything in it belongs to our God. He has prepared this perfect plan for your life. All you have to do is submit and accept it. Soon, you will be in harmony with your Creator, and you will have greater understanding of the verse, "Blessed are the meek: for they shall inherit the earth" (Matt. 5:5).

Chapter 5

WALKING IN THE HIGH CALL OF THE SPIRIT

The voice of him that crieth in the wilderness, Prepare ye the way of the Lord, make straight in the desert a highway for our God.

—Isa. 40:3

Behold, I will do a new thing; now it shall spring forth; shall ye not know it? I will even make a way in the wilderness, and rivers in the desert.

—Isa. 43:19

But the hour cometh, and now is, when the true worshippers shall worship the Father in spirit and in truth: for the Father seeketh such to worship him. God is a Spirit: and they that worship him must worship him in spirit and in truth.

—John 4:23–24

> *I press toward the mark for the prize of the high calling of God in Christ Jesus.*
>
> —Phil. 3:14

A voice cries out from the wilderness of your heart and life, proclaiming, "Prepare ye the way of the Lord." That voice is the voice of the Holy Spirit crying out for your attention. Will you listen to the cry of the Holy Spirit? It is a cry of longing for your heart because your heart was made for him. It is a cry from a jealous Spirit as he longs for a glimmer of your attention. Only he can complete your heart. Can you hear his cry? He cries and cries and cries as a lover does for his lost mate.

> *Wisdom crieth without; she uttereth her voice in the streets: She crieth in the chief place of concourse; in the openings of the gates: in the city she uttereth her words, saying, How long, ye simple ones, will ye love simplicity? And the scorners delight in their scorning, and fools hate knowledge? Turn ye at my reproof: behold, I will pour out my spirit unto you, I will make known my words unto you.*
>
> —Prov. 1:20–23

> *Wisdom is the principal thing; therefore, get wisdom and with all thy getting get understanding.*
>
> —Prov. 4:7

How long will you continue to ignore the voice of God in your life? How long will you continue to be offended by him who loves you? How long will you resist the gentleness of the Holy Spirit? How long will you be wise in your own eyes and continue in your scorning? When will you be ready and willing to answer the call of the mighty Spirit?

Have you ever asked if there was more to God than a religion of do's and don'ts? Is there more to God than just coming to church? God has placed the hunger in your heart because God can answer and satisfy that hunger. God created the deep desire, and God can fill it. God does not want you to live with questions or wander aimlessly in the wilderness of your life. There is a real relationship with God's Spirit that you must discern. Begin to answer the call of the Spirit and all your hungering will be satisfied.

When the Holy Spirit descended on Jesus Christ, he led Jesus Christ to the desert to be tempted and tried by the Devil (Luke 4:1). This is what the Spirit does. He leads us to the desert to be tried and tested by his truth. If we come out victorious, we will come out as Jesus with the blessing and anointing of God upon our lives, and everything we touch will be blessed.

Every time God redeemed his people, he always led them to the desert. When God redeemed Israel from the bondage of Egypt, he led them to the desert. Holy men of old including prophets, anointed kings, John the Baptist, and Jesus Christ were all tested in the desert. The Spirit leads men to the desert where he guides them to all truth and righteousness.

In the Old Testament, God led his people into a physical desert. In the New Testament, God leads us into a spiritual desert that can be found in our hearts and in our lonely prayer closets. When you accept Christ as your Savior, the Spirit will also lead you to a desert. When you submit your soul to Christ and he redeems you, the Spirit will guide you to the desert to teach you truth.

God proved to man that he is able to sustain the lives of a multitude of people in the desert. He proved to all that he is the God of the desert. He proved that he is able to protect his people from vicious armies. He proved that he could send bread from heaven as manna. He proved that he could cause a river to flow from a rock. He proved that he could turn bitter waters to sweet waters. If God provided for all the needs of a multitude of people in the desert then God can take care of you wherever you are.

God brought the children of Israel into the desert to teach them spiritual truths. After they were established in spiritual truths, God brought them into the promise: abundance. God did not bring them into the Promised Land until they understood that it was not the land that sustained them, but God.

The desert is a lonely place because only a few are led by the Spirit, not because God wants it that way but because of the hardness of men's hearts. When it comes to following the Spirit, you will have to walk alone. You cannot hold anyone's hand. This is between you and the Spirit. He will lead you to the desert where all you can do is depend on his presence and his Word.

In the desert you learn to depend totally on God and not on yourself. God becomes everything: the source of your salvation and substance. God will teach you to walk on water, which is a total dependence on his Word. Once you learn that God is your provider then you can enter into his rest and rest from your own works or your own independence. It is in the desert where God becomes God.

In the desert God confronts your reality. In the desert God breaks you. In the desert God reduces you to nothing. God will then take nothing and create something. God took nothing and through his faith he created the universe. God doesn't need our something. God wants our nothing.

In the desert, God will take you under his wings and teach you what is spirit and what is truth. You will be tried and proved by the desert. There the Spirit will reveal to you Jesus—not a girlish man with long hair or a crucified Jesus but an awesome, all-powerful, resurrected Jesus, the Jesus who has fire in his eyes. The Word of God comes out of his mouth as a mighty two-edged sword. You will know that his name is above all and that we exist solely because of his Word (Rev. 1:13–16).

In the desert Elijah, the mighty prophet of God, learned to hear the still small voice of the Spirit. In the desert, he learned to distinguish between emotionalism, fanaticism, flesh, and God (1 Ki. 19:11–13). He learned to be sensitive to the small impressions that the Spirit made upon his spirit.

We are called to learn spiritual truths in the desert. We are taught how to develop that spiritual ability to discern what is spirit and what is truth. We learn to be sensitive to the moving of the Spirit. We learn to be sensitive to what pleases him and continue in it, or we learn what displeases him and remove it from our lives.

In the desert God makes a diamond out of an ordinary rock. Through trials and tribulation, God breaks our character because only through fire does one really know the true substance of his character. Through the process of refining, God establishes the heart in faith, in hope, and in love. In the desert, the Spirit makes a champion out of a willing heart. He forges our character with the fires of God, for God is a consuming fire, and he makes his ministers a flame of fire (Heb. 1:7).

Others have tried to bypass the harshness of the desert. They tried to enter the ministry without first being tested. They have tried to be their own Holy Spirit and establish their own truth. They tried to run ahead of the Spirit instead of being led by the Spirit (Rom. 8:14).

At the first sight of trials and tribulation they were crushed. They live a life of wandering in the desert instead of overcoming the desert. They still live in questions instead of living with truth. They live in self-pity, constantly crying, "Why God? Why me?" They did not learn to commune with the Spirit in the desert. What makes them think they can hear his voice when their boat is rocked, in danger of being sunk?

People who do not submit to the Holy Spirit become merely religious. People who have not been in the desert have not received God's grace. They do not know how to behave among people. They don't know how to serve people and be a proper minister. They are spiritually immature and walk by sight, not by faith. They are weird, bringing attention to themselves by saying how much they hear from God, how many visions and revelations they have. The correct attitude of a spiritual person is not to bring attention to himself but to magnify Jesus Christ.

Finally, you will come out of the desert not with your own opinions but with God's wisdom. You will come out of the desert not trusting in your own abilities but depending on the grace of God. You will come out not with creative man-made solutions but with God's anointing. There is no substitute to God's anointing.

You will come out of the desert with God's stamp of approval from the Holy Spirit. You'll come out with a new heart and new spirit. You'll come out with a tender heart, full of mercy and compassion. You'll come out of the desert not just guessing or confessing that the anointing is on you but knowing that the Spirit is on you. This is where God calls you now.

> *In whom you also trusted, after that ye heard the word of truth, the gospel of your salvation: in whom also after that ye believed, ye were sealed with that holy Spirit of promise, which is the earnest of our inheritance until the redemption of the purchased possession, unto the praise of his glory.*
>
> —Eph. 1:13–14

Are you ready to answer the high call and be led into the desert by the Spirit? Are you ready to enter a higher relationship with God? Are you tired of the shallowness around you? Are you hungry for the living God? Are you ready to live life the way God intended you to live? Are you ready to reach for those things that God has placed before you?

Jesus taught that God is seeking people to worship him in spirit and in truth. God can command people to obey him, but he cannot make them obey. They have a choice. Therefore, God seeks the heart that is willing to obey him.

God is not seeking fanatical people who become religious in their opinions and emotions. God is seeking someone who rests his entire life, health, finances, and future on

God's promises. This is a heart that says, "OK, I only live once. So let's see if you do fulfill your promises. I dare to seek your kingdom and righteousness first above my own will in order to see if you are who you say you are. I want to know that you are God and can provide all my needs!"

God seeks such people who have come to the crossroads of their lives and have no other choice but to choose God, people who have tried everything else but failed miserably. Now they have nothing to lose, so they try it God's way.

These are people who have seen the emptiness of sin and now seek the grace of God. People who have experienced everything else and now are ready to experience the power of God. People who come to God with no more pride but with broken hearts. People who realize that their way hasn't worked, and now they are willing to worship God in spirit and in truth. People who have realized as the disciples once did: "Lord, to whom shall we go? Thou hast the words of eternal life" (John 6:68).

Are you there yet? Have you reached that place in your life?

Jesus said, "The hour cometh and now is." You are living in God's "now is". These are exciting Christian times. The things of God are exciting and challenging. Dead religion is for boring people. God's Spirit is far from dead. Can the church handle such adventures as walking on water? I believe the church is standing at the edge of the boat ready to step out because God has brought us to such a point.

Jesus said that God wants to be worshiped in spirit and in truth. But this is not all. He also mentions a key word that is often overlooked: *must*. They that worship him *must* worship him in spirit and in truth. We can no longer overlook the spiritual laws of God. He will not accept any other forms of worship but the one he has established in his Word. We must worship God the way he wants to be worshipped, in spirit and in truth.

The word *must* is a small word but carries a great concept. The word *must* is defined in *Vines Expository Dictionary* as: (1) it is necessary, there is need of, is right and proper. (c) necessity in reference to what is required to attain some end.

The word *worship* is defined as follows: (1) to kiss the hand to one, in token of reverence, (2) among the Orientals, especially the Persians, to fall upon the knees and touch the ground with the forehead as an expression of profound reverence, (3) in the New Testament by kneeling or prostration to do homage or make obeisance, whether in order to express respect or to make supplication.

Now we can have more insight into what Jesus is trying to convey. In God's wisdom and design, he has established the human heart to need him. In order to fill that need, we must worship him by showing a token of reverence or doing homage to him. Our hearts were designed to be touched by God's Spirit just as our bodies were made to drink water. Our hearts thirst for living waters that only God can provide.

God is Lord. How do you recognize that he is Lord? By worshiping him in spirit and in truth. The highest form of worship is obedience (1 Sam. 15:22). By humbling yourself and obeying his Word, you put his Word above your will, and you are worshiping God in spirit and in truth.

Jesus taught that his words are spirit and truth (John 6:63, 17:17).

The Spirit leads us into the desert to show us truth, so we walk after the Spirit (Rom. 8:1). The Spirit led Jesus because he had a heart and a mindset that pleased God. He followed the Spirit by doing the will of the Father. The Bible teaches us that we have the mind of Christ (1 Cor. 2:16).

Another look into the mind of Christ is this:

> *Let this mind be in you, which was also in Christ, Jesus; Who, being in the form of God, thought it not robbery to be equal with God; but made himself of no reputation, and took upon him the form of a servant, and was made in the likeness of men: and being found in fashion as a man, he humbled himself, and became obedient unto death, even the death of the cross.*
>
> —Phil. 2:5–8

Are you a human being? Then, humble yourself and become of no reputation, take the form of a servant, and become obedient even unto death. If this mind-set was good enough for the Son of God, it is good enough for us. The Father anointed Jesus' attitude with the Holy Spirit, so we will also be anointed by the Father. If this humble attitude pleased the Father and caused him to exalt Jesus, then we, too, will be exalted.

The Spirit first leads us to the desert that we may learn the awesome truth of humbling ourselves (a pleasing worship unto God). Then he will bring us out with exaltation. It is God's desire that we willingly humble ourselves before him and not exalt ourselves, no matter how brilliant our gifts and wisdom may be. It is God who exalts us in due time, not for our glory but for his glory. This must happen before we can be made the head of all things.

> *For whosoever exalteth himself shall be abased; and he that humbleth himself shall be exalted.*
>
> —Luke 14:11

> *Before destruction the heart of man is haughty, and before honour is humility.*
>
> —Prov. 18:12

> *By humility and the fear of the Lord are riches, and honour, and life.*
>
> —Prov. 22:4

> *Humble yourselves therefore under the mighty hand of God, that he may exalt you in due time.*
>
> —1 Pet. 5:6

Out there in the desert, we will find the truth in humility. It is easy to impress people in public with our fancy, stirring prayers. It is easy to impress people with our talents and abilities. It is easy to impress people with our pompous titles and diplomas. It is easy to impress people with our careers and material possessions. However, in the desert there is nobody to impress. In the desert all that remains is you, God, and the truth. How are you going to impress God in the desert?

Many times Jesus departed from the multitude to be alone in the desert, especially when they wanted to make him king. Away from the applause and adoration of people, Jesus found spirit and truth. Jesus said:

> *Therefore when thou doest thine alms, do not sound a trumpet before thee, as the hypocrites do in the synagogues and in the street, that they may have glory of men. Verily I say unto you, They have their reward.*
>
> *But when thou doest alms, let not thy left hand know what thy right hand doeth; that thine alms may be in secret: and thy Father which seeth in secret himself shall reward thee openly. And when thou prayest, thou shalt not be as the hypocrites are: for they love to pray standing in the synagogues and in the corners of the streets, that they may be seen of men.*
>
> *Verily I say unto you they have their reward. But thou, when thou prayest, enter into thy closet, and when thou hast shut thy door, pray to thy Father which is in secret; and thy Father which seeth in secret shall reward thee openly.*
>
> —Matt. 6:2–6

Do you have a prayer closet? Do you know how to pray? Do your prayers impress God? Alone in your prayer closet, can you find God? The Spirit of truth will not accept hypocrisy. The Spirit of truth is not impressed by flesh. Your prayers will never reach God if you try to impress him. The harshness of the desert and its truth confronts your whole philosophy of yourself and life.

You do not come before the presence of God by simply asking. God already knows what you need before you ask

(Matt. 6:8). You come before the presence of God with worship. If your worship is pleasing to God, he will have grace upon you. If you find favor in the eyes of God, he will grant you the desires of your heart (Ps. 37:4).

You must worship God in spirit and in truth. Worshiping God in spirit means that you must understand the voice of your spirit (your conscience). Through your conscience the Holy Spirit guides you to truth. Paul said, "I say the truth in Christ, I lie not, my conscience also bearing me witness in the Holy Ghost" (Rom. 9:1).

Discern the way of the Spirit and the way of truth:

> *Howbeit when he, the Spirit of truth, is come, he will guide you into all truth: for he shall not speak of himself; but whatsoever he shall hear, that shall he speak: and he will shew you things to come.*
>
> —John 16:13

The Holy Spirit will deal with you ever so lovingly, ever so gently. He presses his ways on your heart. For example: When you feel a spirit of heaviness, come to God, and ask if you did something wrong to grieve his Spirit. Examine your heart, and you will find out that you were selfish, judgmental, overly critical, opinionated, or you simply hardened your heart and failed to show kindness and mercy when you could have.

David said, "Judge me, O Lord my God, according to thy righteousness" (Ps. 35:24). A person who desires a deeper walk with the Spirit will ask God to judge him. A person who merely has religion will judge others.

Learn the ways of spirit and truth. When you are in your prayer closet alone with God, you can either worship him in spirit and in truth, or you can simply have no prayer life. You can continue to live in hypocrisy, but you will have no anointing.

God is only impressed by a cry of your spirit. "God, I need you! God, I need you!" Out there in the desert, there is nothing to eat or drink. Out there in the desert, holy men of God cried, "I am hungry for the living God! I am thirsty for your righteousness!"

The desert of truth shrinks a man's self-importance until he realizes that without God, he is nothing. Without his presence upon our lives, we are wretched, poor, blind and naked (Rev. 3:17). "Without you, I am nothing; I know nothing, and I can do nothing!" When you learn to humble yourself in such manner before the Lord, that is worship pleasing unto God!

The act of worshiping God is a way of life that is learned from the Holy Spirit. The act of worshiping God in humility comes from a spiritually mature heart. When we first come to God we are still full of ourselves, but in the process of learning spiritual truths we begin to understand that God is God. We prostrate ourselves before him in worship.

Be sensitive to spiritual things. Everybody lives in the spiritual atmosphere that they have created by their words, their deeds, their thoughts, and their desires. Everyone has a spiritual atmosphere that influences their behavior, moods, and well being. When you understand this concept in your spirit, you will understand the need to worship God. You will understand that in his presence is love, joy, and peace.

Your heart needs these to co-exist in your marriage, at work, at church, and especially within yourself.

God only abides in a contrite or broken heart (Isa. 57:15). Your opinions, criticism, anger, or bitterness only harden your heart and grieve the Spirit of God (Eph. 4:30–31). A broken heart is pleasing unto God. This is the secret place of the holy men of old. This is the secret place of King David and his anointing.

> *O Lord, open thou my lips; and my mouth shall shew forth thy praise. For thou desirest not sacrifice; else would I give it: thou delightest not in burnt offering. The sacrifices of God are a broken spirit: a broken and a contrite heart, O God, thou wilt not despise.*
>
> —Ps. 51:15–17

This wisdom now is handed to you. Only a broken heart knows the correct judgments of God. Jesus said, ". . . and my judgments are just; because I seek not my own will but the will of my Father who has sent me" (John 5:30). People do not have just judgments when they do their own will and seek their own fleshly desires. A broken heart will be given spiritual wisdom to understand life. When your time comes to choose brokenness before God or your own will, what will you choose?

Where will your opinions be when God shakes your foundation? When life spirals out of control, where will your pride be? We speak so arrogantly when we have control, but as soon as our control is gone, our opinions fail. What good are they? Can opinions heal anyone from the coming pestilence? Can opinions change the course of God's hand in nature? Can opinions stop the spirit of disobedience and bitterness that rules in the hearts of many?

The anointing of the mighty Spirit only recognizes one will. The anointing only does the bidding of one will. The anointing flows strong only at the will of God, not the will of man. The anointing will only come upon you when you declare in every situation that comes into your life, "Not my will but your will be done! Thy Kingdom come, thy will be done on earth as it is in heaven!"

You are called to come out of yourself and come into the desert to learn the ways of spirit and truth. You are called to a life of brokenness before God. The choice is yours. God abides in brokenness. If there is no brokenness then the only things that exists are frustration, anger, bitterness, and violence. These are not the ways of God but the ways of flesh and seducing devils.

People will go to the desert to hear such anointed men. In the day of John the Baptist and Jesus, the ministers could not draw crowds to their beautiful, comfortable synagogues. The glory of God had left them. However, under the desert sun on the scorching rocks, people came in great numbers to see the Spirit of God moving through his broken vessels.

Jesus asked about such an anointed man as John the Baptist, "What went ye out into the wilderness for to see? A reed shaken with the wind? But what went ye out for to see?" (Luke 7:24–25). Why do people come to our churches? Do they come simply to be entertained? The world can do a better job of entertaining people than the church can, but what the world cannot do is edify with God's truth. What the world does not have is anointed ministers who know how to edify and equip people's lives (Eph. 4:12).

Ministers represent God on Earth. God is a God of tremendous wisdom and order. How can we bring God down to a level of emotionalism and disorder? It's an insult to God's Spirit when people turn to the soul to find God. God is found on a higher spiritual level that is only attained through a broken heart.

It's an insult to God's Spirit to represent God as simply as an emotional, weird experience. Granted, our first encounter with Christ as our Savior is a dramatic experience in the soul, but afterwards we should be taught how to walk in the Spirit. How will they know, if not through anointed ministers?

God has made man with an intelligent soul. We have to honor and respect God's creation (Matt. 5:22; Jas. 3:9). The church has insulted the intelligence of the world by their soulish acts. It is time for the Christian church to become spiritual and represent God with wisdom and order (1 Cor. 14).

God does marvelous things in the desert. There the Spirit calls to you. God springs forth a new thing in the desert. A river bubbles with life, and it is God's doing.

You are reading this book not by coincidence but by divine appointment. God has placed a hunger for the reality of his person in your heart. The Spirit cries, "Are you ready to come out of the shallows and into the depths of God? Are you ready to understand his ways? Then behold your destiny!"

Understand the Way of the Spirit

You were made for the pleasure of God (Rev. 4:11). Even evildoers were made for the pleasure of God's wrath

(Prov. 16:4). God made some vessels for honor and others for dishonor (Rom. 9:21–23).

Since the beginning of time, God created man to obey his commandments (Gen. 2:16–17; Rev. 1:3). Man has been given the right to choose between obedience and disobedience with results of either blessing or cursing, life or death (Deut. 30:19). God gives everyone a choice to sanctify themselves (1 Thess. 4:4). Therefore, if you obey God you will do his deeds and be called children of God. If you disobey, you will do the deeds of your father, the Devil.

Those who choose to obey God see God as the potter and themselves as the clay. "But now Lord, thou art our father; we are the clay, and thou our potter; and we all are the work of thy hand" (Isa. 64:8). But many choose to resist the ways of God and disobey the ways of the Spirit. "Woe unto him that striveth with his Maker! Let the potsherd strive with the potsherds of the earth. Shall the clay say to him that fashioned it, What makest thou? Or thy work, he hath no hands?" (Isa. 45:9).

With lovingkindness God calls us to be his clay. He asks us to allow him to work in our lives and not to resist his Spirit. "O house of Israel, cannot I do with you as this potter? Saith the Lord. Behold, as the clay is in the potter's hand, so are ye in mine hand, O house of Israel" (Jer. 18:6).

God has everything in control. God knows all our steps. He knows that our ways are foolish and vain. When we ensnare ourselves by foolish decisions, that is where God meets us. Everyone makes foolish decisions. When we are able to understand that we cannot trust in ourselves, God wants us to come to him. He will always accept us, heal us, protect us, renews us, and provide for our needs. Have you reached that level of spiritual understanding to realize that God's ways are the only ways?

How does the Spirit lead us to a desert? God has made life so that sooner or later, our reality is confronted by trouble. Sooner or later we will have a need that only God can answer. Circumstances do not happen by accident. The Spirit of God permits them to come into our lives by divine appointment. Through them, we are tempted, tried, and proved. Through trials and tribulations, God sees if we can come to him and make him our God. It is in our prayer closets where we learn to stay in contact with the spiritual, where we learn to wait upon the mighty invisible hand of God to sustain us.

There are three reasons why a Christian must have trials and tribulations. First: To allow God to mold his character, so he can produce fruit. Second: So he can learn to wait on God and experience his power and know that he is Almighty God. The third reason will be discussed in Chapter 6.

God permits everything that comes into your life so he can mold you into his image. Life has been designed in such a way that God deals with our character through our attitudes, our frustration, our emotions (our entire soul). You can either accept this fact or reject it. If you reject this truth, you have chosen a path of blindness, frustration, and bitterness. If you accept this truth, you have chosen to let God be your potter. You will become clay in his hands, and this verse is yours: "And we know that all things work together for good to them that love God" (Rom. 8:28).

God allows trials in our lives to see if we truly love him, not with lip service but with our hearts. God wants to see if we really believe that he can do what he promised. He leads us to the desert to allow Satan to try us. Our only victory is standing firmly on the Word.

If you place God's Word above your own will, you will begin to see God as a loving father and a strong disciplinary father. A loving father because all his commandments were made for your best interest. A disciplinary father because he will not allow you to reason with him. Once you begin to rely on your own judgments, you are on your own again.

> *My son, despise not thou the chastening of the Lord, nor faint when thou art rebuked of him: For whom the Lord loveth he chasteneth, and scourgeth every son whom he receiveth. If ye endure chastening, God dealeth with you as with sons; for what son is he whom the father chasteneth not? But if ye be without chastisement, whereof all are partakers, then are ye bastards, and not sons. Furthermore we have had fathers of our flesh which corrected us, and we gave them reverence: shall we not much rather be in subjection unto the Father of spirits, and live?*
>
> —Heb. 12:5–9

Chastening and scourging causes suffering. "Though he were a Son, yet learned he obedience by the things which he suffered" (Heb. 5:8). God teaches us obedience through suffering. This is not a very popular statement in today's religion. Please do not stop reading this book. Hear me out, and you will see God's wisdom behind this. This is the truth that is lacking in your life. Just hold on.

Truth cannot be changed or hidden. Truth is a light that cannot be bargained with or smothered because truth is the light of the world. It will shine through eternity. There is no denomination that can change God's Word. There is no fleshly faith preacher that can change this truth. Whether we enter into this or not, it is the Word of God. Now you are confronted with the whole truth.

God is revealing the final truths of his Word, that we may be complete. This is true because it is based on his Word. It is the truth of old that is being restored to the church. With this truth, we will fully understand the dealings of God with man. With this truth, the harmony of the Word of God will come into our beings. It is a central piece to the puzzle of life. The entire Word of God joins to make sense and harmony for he is a God of harmony and order (1 Cor. 14:33,40).

The church of Jesus Christ will become brighter and brighter as the church awakens to truth. People will understand the workings of God in their lives, and they will shine with God's truth. There will be many who teach these things and turn many to righteousness. They will be called great in the kingdom of God (Matt. 5:19).

> *Jesus taught: "I am the true vine, and my Father is the husbandman. Every branch in me that beareth not fruit he taketh away: and every branch that beareth fruit, he purgeth it, that it may bring forth more fruit. Now ye are clean through the word which I have spoken unto you. Abide in me, and I in you. As the branch cannot bear fruit of itself, except ye abide in me.*
>
> —John 15:1–4

Suffering is one way that brings obedience to God's Word (Heb. 2:10). This is not limited to physical suffering.

It is more of a spiritual suffering. Our emotions, our feelings, and our thoughts (our entire soul) will suffer if we are to continue with the ways of the Spirit. We are called to suffering with Jesus Christ. If we are going to obey God's Word over our own will, it makes sense that our soul will suffer as our will is broken.

God will try our emotions, our feelings, our thoughts, our entire being. God will see what we do, how we react when trials and tribulations come. He stretches our soul to the limit over and over again. We must understand that God wants us to submit our being to him through trials and tribulations and allow him to work in our being.

When you are tried, do not hide or run to your reason. Do not hide in your emotions or your feelings. Do not justify yourself. This is flesh, and the Spirit will purge it out. Do not run to man and hide, but run and hide in prayer, in the presence of God until Psalm 91 becomes yours and your secret place is God. After a couple of big trials and tribulations, your entire being will be submitted to God, and he will make you a fortress. You will be a thousand times bigger on the inside than on the outside because his Word has been established in you.

Stop resisting this truth. You are limiting the power of God in your life. The time has come to enter into this new light. "That I may know him, and the power of his resurrection, and the fellowship of his sufferings, being made conformable unto his death" (Phil. 3:10).

Over and over again, God showed Israel that he was able to bring them out of trouble, yet they continued to murmur. When trials and tribulations come into your life, do not murmur or complain. Instead, praise God that he is working in your character and understanding. Do not give in to frustrations or irritations but cast all your cares upon him for he cares for you (1 Pet. 5:7).

When trials and tribulations come your way, let the grace of God be sufficient. In all things let the grace of God be sufficient for your life. When you sense anger or any frustration arising in your heart. Come to God and say, "Give me your grace to learn, to grow, to endure, that I may be established in your ways. Work your ways in me. Let my life please you."

When Jesus told his disciples about his coming suffering, Peter asked him to avoid that path, but Jesus rebuked him saying, ". . . Get thee behind me, Satan: for thou savourest not the things that be of God, but the things that be of men" (Mark 8:33).

When it comes to suffering for Christ, your flesh will rebel against it. Faith preachers may try to preach against it, and many ministers will not understand this path. However, this attitude must be rebuked, for the Holy Spirit is taking the church down this path. Anything that tries to stop you from continuing with God's Spirit must be rebuked. It is of the flesh. Jesus taught everyone to carry his cross and follow him.

> *Take, my brethren, the prophets, who have spoken in the name of the Lord, for an example of suffering affliction, and of patience. Behold, we count them happy which endure. Ye have heard of the patience of Job, and have seen the end of the Lord; that the Lord is very pitiful, and of tender mercy.*
>
> —Jas. 5:10–11

But rejoice, inasmuch as ye are partakers of Christ's sufferings; that, when his glory shall be revealed, ye may be glad also with exceeding joy.

—1 Pet. 4:13

Why are you here on earth? To live life the best way you know how? No. You are here to obey God. In order to obey, God will chasten you. God has chosen to work in your character, to mold your character, and to discipline your character through trials and tribulation. "For even hereunto were ye called: because Christ also suffered for us, leaving us an example, that ye should follow his steps" (1 Pet. 2:21).

God didn't give you faith so you could avoid suffering. He gave you faith so you might understand that God knows what he is doing. He gave you faith so you might know that at the end of this purifying process, God has a far greater reward than whatever you lost or surrendered through trials and tribulations. Through trials and tribulation, you will understand that physical things are not important. Only eternal things are important. He gave you faith to believe and trust in God's process.

For I reckon that the sufferings of this present time are not worthy to be compared with the glory which shall be revealed in us.

—Rom. 8:18

For our light affliction, which is but for a moment worketh for us a far more exceeding and eternal weight of glory.

—2 Cor. 4:17

> *That the trial of your faith, being much more precious than of gold that perisheth, though it be tried with fire, might be found unto praise and honour and glory at the appearing of Jesus Christ.*
>
> —1 Pet. 1:7

The apostles were proud to suffer because all great men of God who were used by the Spirit in the supernatural, suffered for God. The apostles understood that suffering for God brings the comfort of the Spirit.

If there is no suffering, your love for God is only lip service. All you have is religion. However, those who are partakers of the suffering of Christ are partakers also of the consolation of the mighty Holy Spirit. "For as the sufferings of Christ abound in us, so our consolation also aboundeth by Christ" (2 Cor. 1:5).

Jesus Christ taught that the Holy Spirit is the Comforter. If you do not experience suffering, how will you know the Comforter? The greater the suffering, the greater the comfort. When was the last time you experienced the comfort of the Spirit, that wonderful presence that brings love, joy, and peace into our lives? This is what prayer is for, to drink in the presence of the Holy Spirit, who is living water.

Let us grow in the ways of God that we may know how to comfort those with the correct anointing and the correct attitude.

> *Blessed be God, even the Father of our Lord Jesus Christ, the Father of mercies, and the God of all comfort; Who comforted us in all our tribulation, that we may be able to comfort them which are in any trouble, by the comfort wherewith we ourselves are comforted of God.*
>
> —2 Cor. 1:4

This comfort is what the world seeks by fame and fortune. Nevertheless, once they obtained popularity and riches they still don't have peace or joy. They have only emptiness. True joy and peace is only found in the comfort of the presence of God. What the world seeks, only the children of God possess. Love, joy, and peace is only found in the comfort of the Holy Spirit and not in temporal things. Once the apostles learned this secret, they gloried in suffering.

> *We glory in tribulations also: knowing that tribulation worketh patience; and patience, experience; and experience, hope: and hope maketh not ashamed; because the love of God is shed abroad in our hearts by the Holy Ghost which is given unto us.*
>
> —Rom. 5:3–5

The holy men of old gloried in trials and tribulations because they knew God was doing something. In the Old Testament they knew that every time the people of God were tried, God moved in a powerful supernatural way. When the apostles were tried, they raised up their arms in praise because they knew they were about to see the moving of God. That is real faith in a real God!

> *My brethren, count it all joy when ye fall into divers temptations; knowing this, that the trying of your faith worketh patience. But let patience have her perfect work, that ye may be perfect and entire, wanting nothing.*
>
> —Jas. 1:2–4

I lost my job but now I count it all joy because if I had not lost my job I would have never cried unto God and learned how to depend on him. Because I lost my job I learned these spiritual truths. If I had not lost my job, I would never have known God's Spirit and his power. If I had not lost my job, I would have never written this book, and you would not be reading this now. *Thank God for trials and tribulations, I glory in them for everything that comes into my life is permitted by God to work in me a greater truth.*

Through trouble I have learned patience and experienced the power of God. Because I have experienced the power of God, nobody can take this understanding away from me. I have seen the salvation of the Lord, over and over in my life. You too are called to experience the power of God in your life.

God is unfolding his purpose for your life before you. Will you rise up and answer the call of the Spirit? God is not a respecter of persons (Acts 10:34; Rom. 2:11; 1 Pet. 1:17). All he asks is for a willing and trusting heart. He will do the rest, and you will eat the good of the land (Isa. 1:19).

> *But the Lord said unto Samuel, Look not on his countenance, or on the height of his stature; because I have refused him: for the Lord seeth not as man seeth; for man looketh on the outward appearance, but the Lord looketh on the heart.*
>
> —1 Sam. 16:7

On the outside we are different colors, different nationalities, and from different backgrounds. Nevertheless, on the inside we are all the same. It doesn't matter to God if you are short or tall, young or old, ugly or beautiful, thin or chubby, rich or poor. What matters to God is the willingness of your heart to say, "Not my will, but your will be done in my life!"

The prize is set before you, reach out, and take it!

Chapter 6

WALKING DEEPER IN VICTORY

As the hart panteth after the water brooks, so panteth my soul after thee, O God. My soul thirsteth for God, for the living God. . . . Why are thou cast down, O my soul in me? And why art thou disquieted in me? Hope thou in God: for I shall yet praise him for the help of his countenance. . . . Deep calleth unto deep at the noise of thy waterspouts: all thy waves and thy billows are gone over me.

—Ps. 42:1,2,5,7

How far do you want to go with God? There are greater depths in God than you can ever imagine. "O the depth of the riches both of the wisdom and knowledge of God! How unsearchable are his judgments, and his ways past finding out" (Rom. 11:33). Can you handle the deep things of God? This book is only the beginning. This book only shares information, the decision is up to you. Understand this, God put us on earth to discern spiritual things and enter into their depths.

You can discover God through his Word and obedience to his Word and enter into glory and more glory. You can also obey the voice of your uncrucified flesh and the voice of your unrenewed soul and discover the depths of rebellion, pride, selfishness, and depravity. If you choose the voice of flesh, Satan will beguile you and take you into the depth of his kingdom (Rev. 2:24). This is only earthly wisdom and will bring you into spiritual blindness and bondage. It is your decision, but make no mistake, we are either following the ways of God or following the ways of flesh, day by day.

> *Of whom we have many things to say, and hard to be uttered, seeing ye are dull of hearing. For when for the time ye ought to be teachers, ye have need that one teach you again which be the first principles of the oracles of God; and are become such as have need of milk, and not of strong meat. For every one that useth milk is unskillful in the word of righteousness: for he is a babe. But strong meat belongeth to them that are of full age, even those who by reason of use have their senses exercised to discern both good and evil.*
>
> —Heb. 5:11–14

> *But the natural man receiveth not the things of the Spirit of God: for they are foolishness unto him: neither can he know them, because they are spiritually discerned.*
>
> —1 Cor. 2:14

In Chapter 5, we understood the reason why we must be tried. Now, we will go deeper into this spiritual truth. *The third reason for trials and tribulations is to make you weak in yourself so that you can learn to depend and trust in God.*

Can you handle what I just wrote?

Read it again. God designs trials and tribulations to make you weak in yourself so that you may learn to depend and trust in God. *This action of being weak in your abilities also attracts the Spirit of God with great measure.* If you resist the tribulation in your life, you will never be weak. If you are not weak, the power of God will not rest on you.

Let's go back to the teachings of Christ. He gave us early insight into the ways of the Spirit and taught us not to resist trials and tribulations.

> *Ye have heard that it hath been said, An eye for an eye, and a tooth for a tooth: But I say unto you, That ye resist not evil: but whosoever shall smite thee on thy right cheek, turn to him the other also. And if any man will sue thee at the law, and take away thy coat, let him have thy cloke also. And whosoever shall compel thee to go a mile, go with him twain. Give to him that asketh thee, and from him that would borrow of thee turn not thou away.*
>
> —Matt. 5:38–42

All the teachings of Christ are designed to make us weak in ourselves that we may be strong in him and in his Spirit with his grace, power, and anointing. All the teachings of Christ challenge the flesh. Nevertheless, obedience (self-denial) is attractive to the Spirit of God. In other words, things that come naturally to us will only keep us in the natural. Things that do not come natural to us will demand a higher understanding of truth and anointing.

For example: It is natural to walk by sight, but it is supernatural to walk by faith and trust in God. It is natural to be earthly minded and become greedy, but it is supernatural to be eternally minded and live with hope. It is natural to hate your enemies, but it is supernatural to love your enemies. When we obey God, we are no longer walking after the flesh but after the Spirit (Rom. 8:1). When we obey God, we are stepping out of the natural and into the supernatural.

It took me a long time to understand this concept. Now it is in your grasp. God is not in the natural. God is in the supernatural. He is waiting for us to step out of the boat and come to him. God wants people to step out of the natural and live in the supernatural.

Christ brought a new concept to our understanding by teaching us that in the natural there are no spiritual rewards from God.

> *But I say unto you, Love your enemies, bless them that curse you, do good to them that hate you, and pray for them which despitefully use you, and persecute you; That ye may be the children of your Father which is in heaven: for he maketh his sun to rise on the evil and on the good, and sendeth rain on the just and on the unjust. For if ye love them which love you, what reward have ye? do not even the publicans the same? And if ye salute your brethren only, what do ye more than others? do not even the publicans so? Be ye therefore perfect, even as your Father which is in heaven is perfect.*
>
> —Matt. 5:44–48

What benefit is it if we say that we are Christians and do things that are natural? Sinners do that, too. If you dare to obey God, you are walking supernaturally. You will receive a reward because he is a rewarder of those who diligently seek him (Heb. 11:6). The rewards of God are manifold in blessing, in wisdom, and in power. You will also understand that you are in perfect harmony with your Creator. Perfect love casts out torment and fear (1 John 4:18). You will no longer be afraid of evil tidings, of people, of life, or death.

That is why it is so important to read the Bible supernaturally, through God's perspective. If we read the Bible with a natural mind (our point of view), we will never be able to unlock the spiritual truths that take us from glory to glory. Everything we need for life and godliness is already found in the Bible, but these truths need to be spiritually unlocked and understood.

God wants us to live in the supernatural and not in the natural. God wants us to walk on water. In order to walk supernaturally we must live with a broken heart. Now, let us take this a step further. Being broken before God also brings the concept of being weak in ourselves that we may be strong in the Spirit. God delights in our weaknesses so that he may show himself strong in our lives.

This concept appears foolish to the world. To many Christians, also. The world spends a lot of money protecting themselves with lawyers and insurances. To become weak in ourselves is a foolish concept to them. However, when we understand the dynamics behind this concept, we will believe God to take us to a higher level in him.

If we become weak in ourselves, we allow God to be our crusader and Jesus to be our advocate. We give up our limited defenses and allow God to defend us. This attitude permits God to fight our battles, which he so desperately desires to do. He wants to be God in our lives, but first we must step down from the throne.

> *Let no man deceive himself. If any man among you seemeth to be wise in this world, let him become a fool, that he may be wise. For the wisdom of this world is foolishness with God. For it is written, he taketh the wise in their own craftiness. And again, The Lord knoweth the thoughts of the wise, that they are vain. Therefore let no man glory in men. For all things are yours.*
>
> —1 Cor. 13:18–21

Animals are driven by instinct. Men are driven by their reason, and Christians are called to be led by the Spirit (Rom. 8:14). Men have a natural tendency to solve their own problems. Men desire to conquer their world and stay in control. The spiritual force behind this is ego and pride.

The spiritual things of God relate to the condition of man's heart. That's why the Word of God can relate to anyone, at any place, at any time. If pride reigns in his heart then God's presence is far from him. If man humbles himself, God is there to meet him with grace and power.

Allow God to make you weak in the natural that you may experience the power of God in the supernatural. Make yourself weak in yourself that it may be God who gets all the glory. Your weakness is what attracts the power of the Holy Spirit into your life. "Likewise the Spirit also helpeth our infirmities . . ." (Rom. 8:26).

The next time you go through a hard time or an impossible trial, understand that God brought it to your life. He allowed it. All you have to do is stand still and see the salvation of the Lord. Then you will know that he is Lord. He is able to perform great things in your life.

The perfect place for you, is where you are weak in yourself, when things are no longer under your control and you no longer know what to do. When you don't know how in the world you are going to make it, when your only option is to look up and cry unto God—then you will experience the awesomeness of God.

Can you handle such a real relationship with God?

It is natural to depend on a job or salary. It is natural to depend on people and family. It is natural to depend on your intelligence and abilities. When you are laid off or when circumstances spiral out of your control, will you fall apart like the natural man or will you be strong enough to wait on God? It is supernatural to trust in God and wait. That is the challenge of God.

We must see this concept through God's eyes. God can deliver anybody anywhere from anything through a million ways. God is not afraid of anything. God has all power and wisdom. He knows our needs. He wants us to trust in him and to wait on him, so he can establish our hearts. Then we will see his power move in our lives. He may choose to move at the last minute to try our faith, but if we stand our ground we will experience his power.

Are you up to the challenge? Do you have such spiritual guts?

Waiting on God is the hardest thing in the Christian life. God asks us to trust him and place control of our lives in his hands, then live with the spiritual understanding that God is indeed in control.

Can you give up control of physical things? Can you walk on water?

In the past I needed to know that I had all the answers, to feel that I had control over my life. When I was twenty-four, I had already planned out my future, down to the number of children and the cemetery where I would be buried. When the Spirit of God called me into the ministry, I said, “Lord, I already have my own plans. I have a job where I have ten years seniority with benefits, four weeks paid vacation, and a union. The only way I leave is if you somehow kick me out—ha, ha, ha.” One year later I was kicked out. I knew it was God. God shut that door, even though I sought my job with tears—which I am ashamed of now. I did not know then how to wait and trust in God.

> *And Moses said unto the people, Fear ye not, stand still, and see the salvation of the Lord, which he will shew to you to day: for the Egyptians whom ye have seen to day, ye shall see them again no more for ever. The Lord shall fight for you, and ye shall hold your peace.*
>
> —Ex. 14:13–14

> *Be still, and know that I am God: I will be exalted among the heathen, I will be exalted in the earth.*
>
> —Ps. 46:10

Time and time again in the Old and New Testaments, God has brought his people into difficult situations where only he can bring salvation. The Bible is full of such instances to show us that he is able to perform wonders when we trust in him. When the children of God looked to him and not to their own abilities, God brought them out with awesome wonders. That is why Peter praised God in jail. Because God allowed him to be in jail, God could easily deliver him.

Do you want God to do wonders in your life? Can you wait on God and stand on his promises? Life is an adventure with God. He never lets life become boring. He wants nothing to stir your heart but the desire to see a moving of the Holy Spirit.

God will always keep us on the edge of our seats until the supernatural becomes what God always intended: to simply be natural. There is a level in God when faith, hope, and love become natural to the Christian. This is the level of maturity in Christ. This is the level where we strive unto edification.

As Christians, we often have no confidence in our God to stand our ground. We'd rather place our confidence in ourselves. That is why Christians have a hard time even giving their tithes. Start proving God in your life and see that you serve a mighty God. Step out of the boat and begin to walk on water. Learn that nothing is impossible for our God.

> *Bring ye all the tithes into the storehouse, that there may be meat in mine house, and prove me now herewith, saith the Lord of hosts, if I will not open you the windows of heaven, and pour you out a blessing, that there shall not be room enough to receive it.*
>
> —Mal. 3:10

> *And Jesus looking upon them saith, with men it is impossible, but not with God: for with God all things are possible.*
>
> —Mark 10:27

The natural man hates to be weak in himself because he wants to be in control and be his own god. The world cries unto God to take away their trials and tribulations. They become bitter because they do not know the ways of the Spirit. You, on the other hand, are no longer walking naturally but supernaturally. You will shine like the stars because no matter what Satan brings to you to discourage you, it only makes you weak in yourself where God wants you.

> *Who shall separate us from the love of Christ? Shall tribulation, or distress, or persecution, or famine, or nakedness or peril, or sword? As it is written, For thy sake we are killed all the day long; we are accounted as sheep for the slaughter. Nay, in all these things we are more than conquerors through him that loved us. For I am persuaded, that neither death, nor life, nor angels, nor principalities, nor powers, nor things present, nor things to come, nor height, nor depth, nor any other creature, shall be able to separate us from the love of God, which is in Christ Jesus our Lord.*
>
> —Rom. 8:35–39

Are you persuaded, as Paul was, that nothing can defeat you? If you are not convinced, it is because you haven't seen the power of God in your life or because you are still holding onto the temporal. If you haven't seen the power of God in your life, it is because you are not trusting in God. You are only resisting God's Spirit and his ways.

God is not only God of the mountaintop and of the desert. He is also God of the valley. All people want to live on the mountaintop. They always want to feel happy and full of joy. They live by their own truth and motto: "I have a right to be happy." They think that being on the mountaintop is victory. When things do not go their way, they fall to the valley and are depressed. They become bitter and resentful because their fantasy for their lives has not been fulfilled. They will do everything in their power to scurry out of the valley.

Are you ready to understand a beautiful concept? God wants to be God even of the valleys. God wants to meet you there. Do not fight those feelings but tell God that the answer is not in you but in him. Therefore, when you feel weak, depressed, or discouraged, praise God because through your weakness God displays his power. When you find yourself in the valley, tell God that you are trusting in him and not in yourself. Praise God because the answer is not in your abilities but in his abilities. Rest in confidence in God.

> *Yea, though I walk through the valley of the shadow of death, I will fear no evil: for thou art with me; thy rod and thy staff they comfort me. Thou preparest a table before me in the presence of mine enemies: thou anointest my head with oil; my cup runneth over. Surely goodness and mercy shall follow me all the days of my life: and I will dwell in the house of the Lord for ever.*
>
> —Ps. 23:4–6

When you find yourself in an overwhelming situation, praise God! That is the perfect place God wants you. Don't fight it. Don't try to resolve it on your own. Wait on God! Allow him to prove to you that he is God. Just raise your hands in praise, and glory in tribulations because you are about to experience the power of God!

At one time, Paul also fought against the ways of the Spirit. Three times he asked Jesus to take away his trials. But Jesus finally revealed to him a mighty powerful truth, a better way:

> *Of such an one will I glory: yet of myself I will not glory, but in mine infirmities. For though I would desire to glory, I shall not be a fool; for I will say the truth: but now I forbear, lest any man should think of me above that which he seeth me to be, or that he heareth of me. And lest I should be exalted above measure through the abundance of the revelations, there was given to me a thorn in the flesh, the messenger of Satan to buffet me, lest I should be exalted above measure. For this thing I besought the Lord thrice, that it might depart from me. And he said unto me, My grace is sufficient for thee: for my strength is made perfect in weakness . . .*
>
> —2 Cor. 12:5–9

Did you catch that in your spirit? Paul did understand this spiritual concept and once it clicked he declared, "Most gladly therefore will I rather glory in my infirmities, that the power of Christ may rest upon me. Therefore I take pleasure in infirmities, in reproaches, in necessities, in persecutions, in distresses for Christ's sake: for when I am weak then I am strong" (2 Cor. 12:9–10).

When is the Christian strong? When he is weak. The Christian is strong in God when he is weak in himself. Therefore be weak in yourself, in your abilities, in your wisdom, in your solutions. Allow God to work a better way in your life, by depending on his Word. This, My Friend, is taking more steps on water to a greater level of understanding faith.

Learn to distrust what you see. Trust that which cannot be seen. Learn to distrust your reason. Trust his Word which sustains all things. You will live by the confidence of the power of an unseen hand that keeps your life together. It makes perfect sense. God created the physical universe under the laws of faith and grace. He taught us how to apply these laws to our lives. These laws supersede the natural laws because God is God. Therefore, all God requires from you is complete faith in him and his Word. His grace will do the rest.

I do not know how God is going to part the Red Sea to save you. I do not know how God is going to send manna from heaven to feed you and meet your needs. I do not know how God is going to heal you from your sickness. All I know is that he has done it before, he is able to do it now, and he has promised to do it again. Jesus said, ". . . be not afraid, only believe" (Mark 5:36).

How then can the Christian fail? If God desires us to be weak in ourselves and Satan is doing everything in his power to make us weak as he did Job, Paul, and all the holy men of the Bible, then how can we fail? Weakness in ourselves is what God is trying to teach us. When you finally understand it, you will realize that the more this life tries to break you, the more of God rests on you. God has made it impossible for us to ever be defeated.

God has all power and all wisdom. Jesus has triumphed over all things and has placed them at your feet. All you have to do is wait on God and believe.

> *For by him were all things created, that are in heaven, and that are in earth, visible and invisible, whether they be*

thrones, or dominions, or principalities, or powers: all things were created by him, and for him: and he is before all things and by him all things consist, and he is the head of the body, the church: who is the beginning, the firstborn from the dead; that in all things he might have the preeminence.

—Col. 1:16–18

And having spoiled principalities and powers, he made a shew of them openly, triumphing over them in it.

—Col. 2:15

For whatsoever is born of God overcometh the world: and this is the victory that overcometh the world, even our faith.

—1 John 5:4

God has provided a formula so that it will be impossible for you to fail. Instead, you will accomplish great things for God's glory and honor. For example: Let's say you are called to the ministry. This task may overwhelm an individual. However, that is the perfect place God intended for you. The perfect place God wants us to be is when we are weak in ourselves, so God can move and accomplish the task for us. It is no longer our abilities but his abilities through us. We can do all things through Christ who strengths us (Phil. 4:13).

Can you see that it is impossible for a child of God to fail once he understands how God operates? "Now thanks be unto God, which always causeth us to triumph in Christ, and maketh manifest the savour of his knowledge by us in every place" (2 Cor. 2:14).

When we allow God to be God in our lives, we should get ready to walk on water. Who is God in your life? Is it you, your ego? Can you see your error yet? This is what made God angry with the generation of Moses.

> *Harden not your heart, as in the provocation, and as in the day of temptation in the wilderness: when your fathers tempted me, proved me, and saw my work. Forty years long was I grieved with this generation, and said, It is a people that do err in their heart, and they have not known my ways: Unto whom I swore in my wrath that they should not enter into my rest.*
>
> —Ps. 95:8–11

Enter his rest. Take up his offer. This is the deal of your life. Become weak in yourself and turn over your control to God, for he knows all things and sees into your future. Let God now be in control of your life. Jesus said,

> *Come unto me, all ye that labour and are heavy laden, and I will give you rest. Take my yoke upon you, and learn of me; for I am meek and lowly in heart: and ye shall find rest unto your souls. For my yoke is easy, and my burden is light.*
>
> —Matt. 11:28–30

If we follow this line of thought, all of the Word of God will begin to make sense and fall into harmony. This allows us to understand the teachings of Christ through a different perspective.

> *Therefore take no thought, saying, What shall we eat? or, What shall we drink? or, Wherewithal shall we be clothed?*

> *(For after all these things do the Gentiles seek:) for your heavenly Father knoweth that ye have need of all these things. But seek ye first the kingdom of God, and his righteousness; and all these things shall be added unto you.*
>
> —Matt. 6: 31–33

Stop trying to solve everything in your life. Stop trying to solve the problems of your marriage. Instead, become weak in yourself and allow God to try your soul. Give fruit in your marriage. You may say, "I don't love my spouse." Perfect. That is the perfect place God wants you. Now, submit to God, and allow him to break you. Say, "Not my will but your will be done." Soon God will shed his love upon your heart, and you will love your spouse—not with your love but with God's love.

How can this be? How can I love my spouse when I do not feel love? Learn not to be led by feelings. Be led by the Spirit of God. Take the first steps of faith and begin to walk on water. Let your heart love your spouse, and God will meet you halfway. He will keep you on the water. You must first step out of the boat and take the steps on water to experience the reality of God.

If you allow God to work in your life through your spouse, then you will learn to love your spouse unconditionally. It is not your will but God's will. Die to yourself that you may know the resurrection power of God in your life. Put into practice the teachings of Christ. Don't just love when you receive love. Don't just love your mate when your mate does special things for you. What reward is in that? Learn to love your mate unconditionally. Learn to walk in love and be established in it.

Soon the emptiness and frustration will leave. A new power and presence will come into your marriage. It is God! It is God! You will go to church with a new song in your heart. It is God! All I did was submit, and God came in! All I did was rest from my works, and God came in! Praise God! He is mighty! This is what God wants all his children to experience.

Become weak in yourself. Sow weakness in your flesh that you may reap power in the Spirit. "It is sown in dishonour; it is raised in glory: it is sown in weakness; it is raised in power" (1 Cor. 15:43). "God hath chosen the weak things of the world to confound the things which are mighty" (1 Cor. 1:27).

These are the ways of the Spirit. All other ways are the ways of the flesh. This is the high call of God. Keep reaching forward and keep pressing toward. Forget all things that are behind. Don't worry what man thinks or says. Only God is our judge. "For though he was crucified through weakness, yet he liveth by the power of God. For we also are weak in him, but we shall live with him by the power of God toward you. Examine yourselves, whether ye be in the faith; prove your own selves" (2 Cor. 13:4–5).

The heroes of the faith in Hebrews chapter eleven did great things simply by believing in God in the middle of great adversity. God's Spirit declares that the world was not worthy of them. ". . . out of weakness were made strong . . ." (Heb. 11:34). It is your turn for your life to be counted with those that follow after the ways of the Spirit.

This is God's blueprint for our lives. It is a blueprint of everlasting victory. It is a perpetual covenant of triumph.

The more we are tested, the more we submit to God and allow God to purge us. The weaker we become in ourselves, the more the power of God's grace and Spirit shall rest on us until it saturates us and eventually works through us.

When the flesh (our ego) has been dealt with supernaturally, we will understand why the epistles speak of doing things by and through the Spirit. The Spirit will flow in our lives without any obstacles from the flesh. He delights to demonstrate wonders to the world through yielded vessels. He can't wait to show off his power through his church, so that the world can stand in awe and glorify God.

> *Not by might, nor by power, but by my Spirit saith the Lord of hosts.*
>
> —Zech. 4:6

> *In so much that the multitude wondered, when they saw the dumb to speak, the maimed to be whole, the lame to walk, and the blind to see: and they glorified the God of Israel.*
>
> —Matt. 15:31

> *And they were all amazed, and they glorified God, and were filled with fear, saying, We have seen strange things today.*
>
> —Luke 5:26

You were born for such a time as this. Look around you. Sin is rampant, and sin brings people to captivity and death. Will you rise up in this day and hour? Take hold of these spiritual truths and allow God to work in your soul. If you do, people will soon take notice of the work of God in your life and glorify God.

A Biblical Account in 2 Samuel 15 and 16

In the Bible is an account that is a couple of thousand years old. It is as true today as it was back then. We have an example of a mighty man who loved the Spirit and his ways: David.

As a shepherd boy out in the fields, David would meditate on God. He would see the stars in the sky and realize that his God is great. He would play his harp and sing songs to God. Out there in the wilderness with the sheep, he would sing and praise God day after day.

Out there in the desert, alone with the Spirit of God, the cry of his heart was heard in the kingdom of God.

> *O Lord our Lord, how excellent is thy name in all the earth! Who hast set thy glory above the heavens. . . . When I consider thy heavens, the work of thy fingers, the moon and the stars, which thou hast ordained; What is man, that thou art mindful of him? And the son of man, that thou visitest him?... Thou madest him to have dominion over the works of thy hands; thou hast put all things under his feet . . . O Lord our Lord, how excellent is thy name in all the earth!*
>
> —Ps. 8:1,3–4,6,9

Soon, the presence of God began to fall on him. He began to love the presence of the Spirit and began to realize what pleased God. He removed wrong attitudes from his heart. David began to grow strong in the presence of God and in the understanding of the Spirit. He learned to be sensitive to the moving of the Spirit and not grieve the Spirit.

When a bear and a lion came and snatched one of his sheep, the presence of God fell on him. He killed both the lion and the bear. When Goliath defied his God, David went out and killed the giant because he knew God was with him.

David learned to trust God, and God taught David how to rest in him (Ps. 95). Many of David's psalms are about completely trusting God.

After David became king, his son Absalom conspired against him and took his throne by treachery. King David was forced to flee on foot from his kingdom. He told Zadok to carry back the ark of God into the city and added, ". . . if I shall find favour in the eyes of the Lord, he will bring me again, and shew me both it and his habitation" (2 Sam. 15:25) When King David's world was shaken he put his trust in God and not in man. He humbled himself in the sight of God to find his grace and favor.

What should be the reaction of a Christian when he goes through trials and tribulations? "And David went up by the ascent of mount Olivet, and wept as he went up, and had his head covered, and he went barefoot: and all the people that was with him covered every man his head, and they went up, weeping as they went up." (2 Sam. 15:30)

An attitude of humility should be shown to God. This is the correct attitude of worship. David never resisted what God was doing. He always allowed his Spirit to work in his heart a much better way.

Then Shimei, a man of Saul's family, came forth and cursed and threw stones at King David saying,

> *Thou bloody man, and thou man of Belial: The Lord hath returned upon thee all the blood of the house of Saul, in whose stead thou hast reigned; and the Lord hath delivered*

> *the kingdom into the hand of Absalom . . . thou art taken in thy mischief, because thou art a bloody man.*
>
> —2 Sam. 16:5–9

After hearing this, one of David's valiant men said, ". . . Why should this dead dog curse my lord the king? Let me go over, I pray thee, and take off his head" (2 Sam. 16:10).

What would you have done if you were king, your kingdom was snatched away from you, you were fleeing for your life, and then had a bitter person rise up against you and curse you when you were down. If you were a king who killed lions, bears, and giants, and if you led a victorious army through many battles, what would you have done? It would be natural to be filled with pride and take out your frustration upon Shimei. It would have been natural to take off his head and justify it.

> *What have I to do with you, ye sons of Zeruiah? So let him curse, because the Lord hath said unto him, Curse David. Who shall then say, Wherefore hast thou done so? . . . Behold, my son, which came forth of my bowels, seeketh my life: how much more now may this Benjamite do it? Let him alone, and let him curse; for the Lord hath bidden him. It may be that the Lord will look on mine affliction, and that the Lord will requite me good for his cursing this day. And as David and his men went by the way, Shimei went along on the hill's side over against him and cursed as he went, and threw stones at him and cast dust.*
>
> —2 Sam. 16:10–13

David understood the ways of the Spirit. He knew that God permitted trials to test him. He had read the life of Job and studied the ways of God through the Old Testament books that were available; then he personally experienced the presence of God and knew that God allowed this situation. He knew that God could bring him out.

If God brought affliction, it was to teach him obedience and dependence on God. David realized that everything—including his life—was under God's control. David realized that it pleased God when he trusted in him and not in his own strength. He wrote psalms explaining how he lived his life in complete trust in God. David wrote the Third Psalm while he was going through this very experience:

> *But thou, O Lord, art a shield for me; my glory, and the lifter up of mine head. I cried unto the Lord with my voice, and he heard me out of his holy hill. I laid down and slept; I awaked; for the Lord sustained me. I will not be afraid of ten thousands of people, that have set themselves against me round about. Arise, O Lord; save me, O my God. . . . Salvation belongeth unto the Lord.*
>
> —Ps. 3:3–8

When David had the option of killing Shimei, he chose to become weak in himself that God's grace and Spirit may be upon him. He chose to give God control of the circumstances. He allowed God to fight his battles. ". . . that the Lord will look on mine affliction, and that the Lord will requite me good for his cursing this day" (2 Sam. 16:12).

Here we have two lifestyles represented by David and Shimei. These two lifestyles show how the world is divided.

Every one of us is like one or the other. We base our decisions in life on two philosophies. We can react to life's circumstances through the natural way or we can seek God and react to life supernaturally.

In this story, both men lost their titles. Shimei lost his place in royalty when King Saul died, and David took the throne. Shimei lost his privilege. Instead of allowing God to work in him a greater truth, he became bitter. He allowed circumstances to harden his heart against the workings of the Spirit.

Most people either live in the bondage of yesterday or in the vanity of a better future. They do not know how to live in the now. When trials and tribulations come, they become bitter. At the first chance to vent their frustration, they become violent.

However, David knew God and the ways of the Spirit. He waited on God, and God delivered him. Oh, the joy of knowing God and having God fight your battles! O, the peace of resting in God!

> *They that trust in the Lord shall be as mount Zion, which cannot be removed, but abideth for ever.*
>
> —Ps. 125:1

David allowed trials to work in his character. He allowed God to show himself strong in his behalf. Shimei clung to pride and selfishness and only developed an empty heart.

Which lifestyle do you choose?

When David's son Solomon became king, one of the first things he did was to confront Shimei (1 Ki. 2:36–46).

Eventually he took off Shemei's head because Shimei dared to curse the anointing of God instead of doing homage.

You can allow trials and tribulations to work in you by God's way, or you can simply become bitter and empty. You can fight the workings of God and join the multitudes of people who only curse God and die. Bitter people are worthless. All they do is use up God's air.

Jesus said,

> *Ye are the salt of the earth: but if the salt have lost his savour, wherewith shall it be salted? It is thenceforth good for nothing, but to be cast out, and to be trodden under foot of men. . . . Let your light so shine before men, that they may see your good works, and glorify your Father which is in heaven.*
>
> —Matt. 5:13,15

Chapter 7

REASON DROWNS THE HEARTS OF MEN

And be ye not conformed to this world: but be ye transformed . . .

—Rom. 12:2

Peter asked Jesus to let him walk on water. Man will always ask to walk in the supernatural. God will always answer, "Come." God is always ready to walk on water. Man is not. Many people want to walk on water, but few take the time and effort to understand what it takes to stay on the surface.

Peter took a couple of steps on the water before his mind exploded with reasons why this was an impossible feat. He looked to the physical—the wind and the waves—and the physical confirmed his reasoning. Then he began to sink.

Jesus grabbed Peter and asked, "Why did you doubt?" (Matt. 14:31). Jesus knows exactly what causes man to doubt and then to sink. Jesus asked this question so Peter could meditate on the question and come to grips with the answer. Once man understands the answer with his heart, he can freely walk on water.

What holds people from advancing to great heights in the presence of God? What has stopped the power of the Holy Spirit from reaching the hearts of men? Reason. What has calloused the hearts of men against God's truth? Reason. What has stunted people from growing from faith to faith and glory to glory? Reason. What has blinded Christians from obtaining the spiritual level of the apostles? Reason. What is your only true enemy? Your reason.

> *And might not be as their fathers, a stubborn and rebellious generation; a generation that set not their heart aright, and whose spirit was not steadfast with God. . . . Yea, they spake against God; they said, Can God furnish a table in the wilderness? Behold, he smote the rock, that the waters gushed out, and the streams overflowed; can he give bread also? Can he provide flesh for his people? Therefore the Lord heard this, and was wroth. . . . Because they believed not in God, and trusted not in his salvation. . . . How oft did they provoke him in the wilderness, and grieve him in the desert! Yea, they turned back and tempted God, and limited the Holy One of Israel.*
>
> —Ps. 78:8,19–22,40–41

They asked, "Can God provide for our needs?" Reason always starts with a question that defies the power of God. Natural reason will always defy the Word of God. Natural men will always find a witness in the natural to stand against God's promises and limit the power of the Holy One in their lives. In the natural, their reason has been established and now stands as a stronghold against them.

In the history of inventions and aviation, natural men thought it was impossible to do certain things, such as to fly. However, when men discerned the laws of aviation, they soon learned to fly. Once man attained knowledge, they used that knowledge as a key to open doors and unlock certain mysteries. The same thing happens with the things of God. It is just a matter of time before spiritual men discern the spiritual laws that govern our lives and the physical world around us. Once they discover spiritual laws, the Word of God and the Spirit of God become very real and reasonable. My quest is to prove to you that spiritual things are more reasonable than anything else.

God calls us to walk on water. He defies our reason and logic and dares us to trust him. He challenges us to walk by faith and not by sight (2 Cor. 5:7). He delights in our inward ability to obey his Word more than our own reason. He desires for us to trust less in our reason and more in the power of his Word. He challenges us to first believe and then we will see. Yet, many of us are stuck at the threshold of faith. We want to first see and then believe. We want to live by sight, feelings, emotions, and thoughts instead of by God's Word.

God's Word and man's reason will always meet at a crossroad where man must choose. Of course, if man does not know God and his ways, it is obvious that man will choose his own reason.

Since the beginning of mankind, Satan has placed doubt in God's Word. That is all Satan can do—lie and pervert the truth. Satan contradicted God's Word and lured Eve to trust her reason instead of God's Word. He is the Devil and the deceiver of nations. He sows doubt in God's Word by way of reason.

> *Yea, hath God said, ye shall not eat of every tree of the garden? . . . the woman said, We may eat of the fruit of the trees of the garden: but of the fruit of the tree which is in the midst of the garden, God hath said, Ye shall not eat of it, neither shall ye touch it, lest ye die. And the serpent said unto the woman, Ye shall not surely die: For God doth know that in the day ye eat thereof, then your eyes shall be opened, and ye shall be as gods, knowing good and evil. And when the women saw that the tree was good for food, and that it was pleasant to the eyes, and a tree to be desired to make one wise, she took of the fruit thereof, and did eat, and gave also unto her husband with her; and he did eat.*
>
> —Gen. 3:1–6

Eve saw that the fruit was good for food and that it was pleasant to the eyes. She began to contemplate on the forbidden fruit until her reason gave way to desire as another spiritual force came into her heart. Then she took the fruit and ate it. The Devil planted seeds of doubt in Eve's heart until weeds of reason sprang forth. With time, weeds of reason choked the Word of God in the heart.

After Eve ate the fruit and sinned against God, she deceived her husband. Instead of speaking God's Word, she spoke Satan's word to her husband. Whose word are we believing and preaching to others?

Since Eve, all that man has done is reason against God's Word. Man became temporal, shortsighted, and vain. Then, God's Spirit began to search the earth for hearts that dared to believe in the power of his Word rather than their own reason.

In the beginning was the Word (John 1:1). In the beginning there only existed the will of God. Evil is doing another will. When rebellion came into the created beings (man) they rejected the same Word that made them. They began to do their own will. This drove them into darkness. Their flesh and their understanding became darkened.

Then, according to the predestined will of God, his Word became flesh and dwelled among his created beings. He began to call men out of their darkness and into his light. However, man knew only darkness. Man found it hard to comprehend the light. His heart was still darkened with evil.

"But I fear, lest by any means, as the serpent beguiled Eve, through his subtlety, so your minds should not be corrupted from the simplicity that is in Christ" (2 Cor. 11:3).

Satan's only tactic is to lie through reason. If your mind accepts his reason, his reason corrupts you. However, truth will always remain. Once you understand this, the truth will set you free. Darkness can never prevail because light conquers darkness.

God told one-hundred-year-old Abraham that he was going to be the father of a multitude of people. When Abraham heard that he was going to have a child through Sarah, he laughed (Gen. 17:17). Sarah also laughed.

"Now Abraham and Sarah were old and well stricken in age; and it ceased to be with Sarah after the manner of women. Therefore Sarah laughed within herself, saying, after I am waxed old shall I have pleasure, my lord being old also?" (Gen. 18:11–12).

Sarah's reason knew that it was impossible for her to give birth. She focused on the natural and not on the supernatural. She focused on herself and not on the power of God. The only thing reason does is focus on the natural. Therefore, God asked why she laughed. God said, ". . . is any thing too hard for the Lord?" (Gen. 18:14).

To trust the power of God more than one's reason is the way of the Lord. God not only taught Abraham the way of faith but also how to depend on the power of God. You must understand the way of the Lord. It is powerful far beyond one's reason. ". . . and they shall keep the way of the Lord, to do justice and judgment . . ." (Gen. 18:19).

God promised to make Abraham a father of a multitude of people through Isaac. After seeing the birth of Isaac, Abraham definitely knew that nothing was impossible for God. He understood that God's Word is more powerful than the physical. Abraham realized that God's covenant was sure and unbreakable.

When God asked Abraham to sacrifice his only beloved son, Abraham woke up early in the morning to obey God. Abraham's heart had only a strong will to obey God no matter what God commanded. His heart was poised to see a moving of God or to behold an awesome miracle. Abraham knew that Almighty God had made him a promise. Abraham knew that if he sacrificed Isaac as a burnt offering, that God was powerful enough to bring Isaac back from the ashes.

We must also learn to crave a moving of God. We must look at this life as an opportunity to behold a miracle. We must obey God's Word so that power and miracles may come into our lives.

Through this story, we catch a glimpse into God's viewpoint of man and life. God wants man to completely understand that God's Word is final in any given situation. That is where God wants us: to know and depend on the power of God's Word.

"By faith Abraham, when he was tried, offered up Isaac: and he that had received the promises offered up his only begotten son, Of whom it was said, That in Isaac shall thy seed be called: Accounting that God was able to raise him up, even from the dead" (Heb. 11:17–19).

Esau was the firstborn of Isaac. Therefore, Esau had the birthright and the blessing of his father. Yet, when he was hungry he sold his birthright to his younger brother, Jacob, for food because he reasoned, "Behold, I am at the point of death; and what profit shall this birthright do to me?" (Gen. 25:32). Many people are reasoning away their birthright in Jesus Christ. Our inheritance is mighty in Jesus Christ, yet because the temporal is so real to us, we lose our birthright to reason.

Captain Naaman almost lost his healing because of reason and anger. Elisha told the proud captain to submerge in the waters of Jordan seven times. Captain Naaman was offended because the man of God sent a servant instead of coming out to speak to him.

> *But Naaman was wroth, and went away, and said, Behold, I thought, he will surely come out to me, and stand, and call on the name of the Lord his God, and strike his hand over*

the place, and recover the leper. Are not Abana and Pharpar, rivers of Damascus, better than all the waters of Israel?

—2 Ki. 5:10–14

Reason and anger almost robbed Naaman from his healing, but when he obeyed the man of God, he was healed.

When Jesus was teaching and preaching, the chief priests, the scribes, and the elders came to Jesus and asked him questions, trying to trap him. When he responded with a question of his own, they reasoned among themselves: "The Baptism of John, whence was it? From heaven, or of men? And they reasoned with themselves, saying, If we shall say, From heaven; he will say unto us, Why did ye not then believe him? But if we shall say, Of men; we fear the people; for all hold John as a prophet" (Matt. 21:24–25).

Jesus asked the chief priests and the elders where John the Baptist received his spiritual wisdom: from heaven or from men? From heaven comes the revelation of God's Word to the heart of the believer, creating a born-again creature of light. From men come reasons of the flesh to trap man's soul with tradition, philosophy, and temporal things.

Men reason in their hearts until their hearts harden against God's power. It is God's desire and purpose that all men be saved. When men harden their hearts, not even God can save them with all his power and wisdom. This can be seen in a parable of Jesus as the sower and the seed (Matt. 13).

Understand that you are the one who limits the power of God in your life. God has done everything to ensure that you have complete access to his throne. He sacrificed his only beloved Son to do so. God has made sure that not even sin can stop you from coming to him.

The only thing that stops you from coming to him is your own reason. Your reason has created strongholds around your heart that limit the Word of God. Your reason has created arguments in your life that defy the living God.

The works of reason are doubt and fear. They will destroy you spiritually, mentally, and physically. God made you to live by faith on his Word. If you have no faith, then stress—a product of worry or fear—will be your companion.

Doubt and fear are negative spiritual forces that will consume your mind and body. Your mind and body were not made to cope with these forces. Your mind and body were made to function with faith, hope, and love.

Two wisdoms in the world

Satan's wisdom is earthly and sensual (Jas. 3:15). "But the wisdom that is from above is first pure, then peaceable, gentle, and easy to be entreated, full of mercy and good fruits, without partiality, and without hypocrisy" (Jas. 3:17).

When man is born he learns to understand this world through the five physical senses. He learns to rely on his five senses for input or perception. When man is born again by accepting Jesus into his heart, he begins to understand everything through God's Word, which is revealed to his spirit (Matt. 16:17). This is the highest form of wisdom because it is eternal.

Spiritual wisdom teaches man to live for the eternal and not for the temporal. In other words, this wisdom teaches us to not live for the present issues of pleasures and sin but for that unique moment when we stand before God in judgment.

Without God, men understand life only through their perception. They live life with the best reason they can muster. They depend more on their reason than on God's Word. They are only aware of their five physical senses and are not spiritually sensitive enough to hear their God-given conscience.

The more they grow in the wisdom of their own reason, the more other men of reason compliment them. To men, the highest form of wisdom is making money and being self-reliant. However, Satan has crept into their understanding and has taken men into a different path. Satan has told men, "See, you do not need God. You can exist on your own."

The wisdom of this world is foolishness to God because God made life in such a way that it only works through his grace or power. God made marriage in such a way that it only works with his grace, not through man's wisdom.

The foolish wisdom of this world is men trying to solve their own problems. Man wants to be his own god and be self-providing, self-reliant, and self-evolving. That is where God catches the crafty in his own craftiness. *Life was not meant to be lived without God's grace. Life without God has no meaning or value.*

Satan has manipulated the wisdom of this world to be shortsighted, temporal, and selfish. Without revelation knowledge of God's Word, men are simply guided by their own corruptible reason. Through men's reason, the Devil knows how to pervert their hearts. Through reason, men have learned to walk by sight.

We all live in two worlds: physical and spiritual. The spiritual world cannot be seen with our human eye. Jesus said, "That which is born of the flesh is flesh; and that which is born of the Spirit is spirit" (John 3:6). The physical came from the spiritual. The spiritual is more real, more powerful than the physical and governs the physical. The spiritual world is all around us and within us.

Even if you are an atheist, there is a spiritual world within you that controls your life. This spiritual world is made up of so many voices. "There are, it may be, so many kinds of voices in the world, and none of them is without signification" (1 Cor. 14:10).

These voices that come from inside of us are our thoughts, our feelings, our desires, our emotions, our ego, our conscience, and demonic influences. Our reason tries to follow the best voice that makes the best sense at every moment. The only voice that pleases God is the voice of our conscience that is guided by the Holy Spirit of truth.

The spiritual world controls the physical. Everything that was made in the physical, first began with a thought. It is the unseen that already controls our lives. The spiritual world within us is made of voices that we constantly hear and obey. A spiritual man is someone who discerns these voices from within and obeys only the conscience guided by God's Word and the Holy Spirit.

Whether you like it or not, you are more spiritual than you think. The body can be dissected but you will never see a thought, a feeling, or an emotion. However, just because you cannot physically see them—it does not mean they do not exist. You do not have to see a thought to know that it exists. You know it exists and it controls your life.

You are made from the spiritual. The spiritual created your spirit, soul, and body. God spoke, and man came into being. The Word of God made you. When you accept the Word of God into your heart, you are spiritually born again. You crave spiritual wisdom and understanding.

You came from God who is a Spirit. You have the potential within you to believe and trust God's Word. The Word of God already sustains the universe. If you accept Jesus Christ into your heart and obey his Word, the Word will sustain your inward being.

Satan's only objective is to stop you from obeying the Word. He has taught man to trust in his own heart, in so-called gurus, in self-help books, in the wisdom of man, and in his own positive thinking. God says, "Trust in the Lord with all thine heart and lean not on thy own understanding. In all thy ways acknowledge him, and he shall direct thy paths. Be not wise in thine own eyes: fear the Lord and depart from evil" (Prov. 3:5–7).

I try not to be narrow-minded but open-minded. I don't close myself to self-help books. There is a lot of wisdom in those books, and they do help people. Self-help books are all written by men who have learned a certain truth. However, revelation knowledge is on a higher level. It's more powerful than our own minds. Nothing will ever compare to the power of God's grace. His grace is on a higher level than our own abilities.

In other words, self-help books and gurus teach you to be confident in your own abilities. The Word of God teaches us to be confident in him. That is a higher level of power and wisdom beyond our own abilities.

You need to trust God completely. You cannot even trust in your own heart because Satan can use your heart to deceive you. He will make anything appear to be good and deceive you. He will paint a beautiful picture before you but will never tell you that the final outcome will be sin, emptiness, and death. God's Word is the only thing you can trust.

Therefore, obey God above your own heart. "The heart is deceitful above all things, and desperately wicked: who can know it?" (Jer. 17:9). "Keep thy heart with all diligence; for out of it are the issues of life" (Prov. 4:23).

There is a demonic spiritual force at work in the world. It deceives the hearts of people and keeps them spiritually ignorant of God's Word. "In whom the god of this world hath blinded the minds of them which believe not, lest the light of the glorious gospel of Christ, who is the image of God, would shine unto them" (2 Cor. 4:4).

Even if God would again part the Red Sea with national television crews there, so all could watch, people would still refuse to give their hearts to Jesus. Why is this? Because people do not know how. They do not understand the beauty and the awesomeness in God. They would prefer to go to hell for eternity than to give up their sinful lifestyles. They love darkness more than the light. They will go after the flesh rather than put away childish things and repent.

Even if you had an incredible spiritual experience, the process of having a spiritual walk with God is still the same. Even if you search all truth and discover that God does exist and he is who he says he is, you still need to surrender your life to him.

Once you have done your research as I prescribe in Chapter One, and you are convinced that God does exist, what's the next step? You still have to submit your inward being to God and begin a real relationship with your Maker. Whether you have an incredible experience in God or not, everyone still has to submit his soul to Jesus Christ.

Let me give you a short description of man's heart. First, we are born by flesh and begin to live our lives by reason. The majority of people live in reason—including many Christian people. From the point of reason, we are constantly making decisions from the spiritual world within us. These decisions will either spiritually bless or curse our lives.

All of humanity who have lived on earth—past, present, and future—are in the palm of God's hand. God understands exactly how man's reasoning works.

God understands exactly who you are. He thoroughly understands how your heart is made, and he knows the final outcome of your life. Through revelation knowledge of his Word, he wants to help you find your path in life.

Men who follow the ways of reason become overly sensitive, emotional, and insecure. Reason will always make men resemble the waves of the ocean: double minded. They say one thing, but later their reason will talk them out of it. God will plant his Word in their hearts, and later their reason will pluck it out. "But let him ask in faith, nothing wavering. For he that wavereth is like a wave of the sea driven with the wind and tossed. For let not that man think that he shall receive any thing of the Lord. A double minded man is unstable in all his ways" (Jas. 1:6–8).

The only thing a man of reason does is play games. He plays games with himself, with others, and with God. No one depends on his word, and no one trusts him. His employer cannot promote him because he is unstable.

Men of reason smile in your face and stab you in the back. Men of reason lie to you in order to receive a vote. Men of reason believe that you have to step on people and use people to get somewhere. Men of reason think they are so smart that their own abilities have gained them prestige. They hold high and powerful positions because they have sold their souls to the Devil. Their reason has taken them to the path of lies and deception.

If you are a business executive or politician or in any career that depends on your selling your soul to treachery, quit. There is a place in hell where the rivers run hot, set aside for business people, politicians, lawyers, and anyone else who brings offenses into the world. Jesus said, "And if thy hand offend thee, cut if off; it is better for thee to enter into life maimed, than having two hands to go into hell, into the fire that never shall be quenched" (Mark 9:43).

Your conscience has dealt with you along these lines already. You know it is true. If it is in your power to do right, do it. Your reward in heaven and also here on earth will be great. "Therefore to him that knoweth to do good, and doeth it not, to him it is sin" (Jas. 4:17).

Let us take a closer look at what happens in a man's life when he does not obey God's Word. For example: Instead of bringing his thoughts into captivity to the obedience of Jesus Christ, a man allows that thought to grow into imaginations. He begins to relish his imaginations until the lust it produces is satisfied in his flesh. Every time he relishes that thought, the desire grows for more satisfaction.

The Word of God says, "Casting down imaginations, and every high thing that exalteth itself against the knowledge of God, and bringing into captivity every thought to the obedience of Christ" (2 Cor. 10:5). If you do not cast down imaginations, your only other option is to be a slave of your imaginations, ". . . but became vain in their imaginations, and their foolish heart was darkened. Professing themselves to be wise, they became fools" (Rom. 1:21–22).

The flesh has no limits. It will always crave more and more. Soon, men are no longer in control of their thoughts or of their lives. Lust drives them deeper into depravity. They do not understand what is happening to them. All they know is that lust controls them, and they can't stop themselves.

What first started as an uncontrolled thought grew into lust of the flesh, which led them into sexual bondage. When normal sex did not satisfy them, weird sexual things became an alternative. There is no end to the perversion that can develop. The flesh will crave different things, always stretching the limits of depravity to fill the ever-growing void.

At this point, they cannot stop. They know what they're doing is wrong, but they continue to surround themselves with others who encourage them, or they surround themselves with demons who encourage them. Lust as an evil spirit takes over their lives, and they have no power against it. A seducing spirit has captured their minds, and they are now bound to its will (1 Tim. 4:1; Rom. 6:16).

That is what Satan does with his demons—perverts the heart that opens its door to them. They will pervert all that is holy in the eyes of God. Satan will use man to mock God. They don't realize that they are slaves to evil influences. After their perversion is satisfied, emptiness remains in their hearts.

Others live by their feelings. Feelings lead them into captivity and make them victims. Do not listen or give in to feelings. Do not wear your feelings on your sleeve. Do not become sensitive to people's remarks or attitudes against you. God has not called you to be a victim but victorious in Christ Jesus. Submit those feelings to God and walk in love.

It is a privilege and an honor to submit our emotions to God. There is no other God in the world who loves us. We can take our feelings, thoughts, and emotions to him. He gives us rest, peace, and wisdom. What does the world have? How can they cope with their emotions? They are irritated, frustrated, and angry. They take out their emotions and frustrations on each other. They are part of a vicious cycle. They are empty and they are searching for fulfillment outside of God.

Another tactic of Satan is to deceive people into believing that they are wiser than God. They become cynical and sarcastic. They think they are so wise in themselves that they can read people's hearts and motives. For them, everyone has a hidden agenda. Everyone is out to get rich, or everyone is out to get them. Everything is a conspiracy. They are so smart and self-reliant that they do not need God.

However, I ask, have you ever made a mistake in your life? Look at your life. Are you sure you can trust yourself and your judgments? Are you sure you are always correct? Are you sure this cynical, sarcastic attitude has not blinded you? Are you sure this attitude has not deceived you into believing that everyone else is wrong except you? Are you sure disobedience to God's Word is better than obedience? If you made a mistake before, can it be possible that you are now making the biggest mistake of your life by not accepting Jesus Christ as Lord of your life?

You are so wise that you do not need God. How exactly do you know that you are wise? To whom do you compare yourself? Who told you that you are wise? Was it your beer-drinking buddies or because you know how to make money? Wake up. Satan is a serpent, and he is so subtle.

Another demonic voice that man hears is Satan with his earthly wisdom. He whispers in your ear that you are not complete, that you need something or someone to fill the growing void in your heart. His wisdom is powerful and has deceived many more people than the gospel of Jesus Christ has liberated. However, that is going to change in my generation!

All of Satan's wisdom only leaves you dirty and empty. As a Christian you need to stand up against those lies of the Devil and declare the Word of God! Say, I am complete in Jesus Christ! I do not need another lover or anything from this world!

> *Beware lest any man spoil you though philosophy and vain deceit, after the tradition of men, after the rudiments of the world, and not after Christ. For in him dwelleth all the fullness of the Godhead bodily. And ye are complete in him . . .*
>
> —Col. 2:8–10

Tell the Devil that he can keep his lies in hell because you know the truth. It is written that you are complete in Christ Jesus! Once you realize the truth that you are complete only in your Creator, you will seek him to fill the void. Realize that the power of Jesus Christ is in you to bring every thought into captivity. In time you will realize that his power is changing you. The power of the Holy Spirit will fill the void that was in your life. The more you trust him with your life, with your thoughts, with your feelings, with your emotions, the more he will trust you with his power. Jesus will truly become the Lord of your life.

The only thing Satan wants to do is manipulate your life and use it for his selfish purpose: to mock God. He will pervert you, so he can laugh at God: "See God, he obeys me more than your word. He does my will!"

Once he is done with a man's life, Satan will discard him as a dirty rag. Satan deceives an individual, as perverted men deceive women through lies, through deception, through violence and—after they are done—they discard them like a piece of garbage. People all over the world feel that their lives are empty, worthless, and meaningless because they allowed Satan to deceive and use them.

The world has decided to reject the ways of the Spirit. Instead of walking in love, they walk in selfishness. Does the world really think they can simply disobey God and nothing will happen to them? The world woke up and realized that the Holy Spirit has departed from their lives, and an evil spirit remains.

A spiritual curse has gone forth into the land. This curse is now at work in the hearts of many. This curse has many facets, especially a feeling of emptiness. This curse is weighing right now upon the lives of many people. Men are coming to the understanding that life without God is worthless.

The world is trying to run away from such emptiness. They try to drown that feeling with alcohol. They try to dance and party the night away, but their emptiness remains. They do not know how to escape from the curse. They turn to every fleshly satisfaction imaginable, but there is no release or comfort.

Reality is the truth of God that they are trying to elude. This spiritual reality testifies in their hearts that they are nothing, and their lives are meaningless. It is not a chemical imbalance. It is not a mental disorder. It is not a psychology thing. It is not because life has been so unfair. It is a spiritual thing. It is a heart thing. It is a conscience thing. It is a God thing. It is a spiritual truth, an eternal truth that will never change but will remain forever. The Word of God is truth. The Word declares that if you are not walking in love YOU ARE NOTHING! (1 Cor. 13:1–4). If you lost your Christian joy, YOU ARE WORTHLESS! (Matt. 5:13).

Through his great grace and mercy, God can come down to any level where man is and bring him out of that sin. God can come down to the level of reason and reason with man. "Come now, and let us reason together, saith the Lord: though your sins be as scarlet, they shall be as white as snow; though they be red like crimson, they shall be as wool. If ye be willing and obedient, ye shall eat the good of the land" (Isa. 1:18–19).

You need to recognize that the only power that can help you is the Holy Spirit. Drop onto your knees, and cry out to

God for help. Submit your thoughts to him. He will never reject you. "Then they cry unto the Lord in their trouble, and he saveth them out of their distresses" (Ps. 107:19). "Call unto me, and I will answer thee, and shew thee great and mighty things, which thou knowest not" (Jer. 33:3).

You will declare as King David did, "He brought me up also out of an horrible pit, out of the miry clay, and set my feet upon a rock, and established my goings. And he hath put a new song in my mouth, even praise unto our God" (Ps. 40:2–3).

Reason within Christian circles

Saul, who later became the apostle Paul, had great zeal for God. In his zeal for God he began to persecute the Christian church, believing he was right.

> *Concerning zeal, persecuting the church; touching the righteousness which is in the law, blameless, but what things were gain to me, those I counted loss for Christ. Yea doubtless, and I count all things but loss for the excellency of the knowledge of Christ Jesus my Lord: for whom I have suffered the loss of all things, and do count them but dung, that I may win Christ and be found in him, not having mine own righteousness . . . but that which is through the faith of Christ, the righteousness which is of God by faith.*
>
> —Phil. 3:6–9

Jesus revealed himself to Saul and asked Saul why he was persecuting Jesus (Acts 9:4–5). Saul was trying to do something for God with his own wisdom and strength. However, instead of helping he was hurting the cause of

God. Saul repented and became known as Paul, a prisoner of Jesus Christ. Without spiritual knowledge, like Saul, we may also be hurting the cause of God.

God is preparing to move in the latter rain. Every time his Spirit moved with great anointing, Satan also moved in the flesh with great hypocrisy. Therefore, not only do we have to teach people how to let the Spirit lead them, but we must also teach people how to stop the flesh from leading them.

Satan has moved in the flesh with the pride of men to deceive and to bring a reproach on the moving of God. However, won't we be ready this time? Won't we recognize what is Spirit and what is flesh?

Throughout time, Christians have searched for God. Those who submitted their entire beings to God moved with the wisdom and power of his Spirit. Those who did not know how to submit still had zeal to do something for God. Being zealous for God is good, but being zealous without knowledge is wrong. "For I bear them record that they have zeal of God, but not according to knowledge" (Rom. 10:2).

For two thousand years, men have tried to do spiritual things through their own understanding and through their own strengths. Many men and churches have done horrible things in the name of God. They have dominated, killed, robbed, lied, and have done every abominable thing. This is what happens when men do not allow the Spirit to lead them. The ways of men are not the ways of God but usually result in the ways of a highly seductive and deceitful Devil.

Many Christians have great zeal and are trying to do something for God. Some are trying to force the fire to come down from heaven with their own abilities and wisdom. They are desperately trying to force a moving of God. This is only flesh, and God sees it as hypocrisy.

It is natural to rely on our own wisdom and abilities rather then on God's power. It is spiritual maturity to rely on God and not ourselves. The Word of God is on a higher spiritual plane. We must fall to our knees and seek that higher wisdom. Otherwise, we will rely on our own wisdom and make the Word of God of no effect. We will be resisting the Spirit of God instead of being blessed. This only produces frustration. However, everything becomes simple when we allow the Spirit to break us.

Many Christians use the Word of God as a reference to their thoughts and ideas. We cannot take the Word of God, mix it with our reason, and expect God to bless the outcome. This perverts the Word of God, and we are no longer ministers of God's Word. We become ministers of our own words, and that is satanic in nature. This, in turn, creates legalism, religion, fanaticism, and denominations.

Much of the Christian mentality is to trust in professional men instead of God's anointing. The Christian world has learned to trust experts, doctors, educators, and politicians, rather than the Holy Spirit.

Denying your inward being and bringing it into captivity to the obedience of Jesus Christ may go against conventional wisdom, but I have news for you: Conventional wisdom isn't working. Sin is rampant. These intellectual men appear to have the answers, but without God they are only deceiving and being deceived (2 Tim. 3:13).

You think your reason can break the yoke of bondage? Did Jesus call us to preach the gospel to the poor with reason? To heal the brokenhearted in our reason? To preach deliverance to the captives with our reason? Recover the sight of the blind by reason? To set at liberty them that are bruised through reason? No sir! Reason is of the flesh. God doesn't need our reason. We are called to do things by the anointing of God's Spirit.

Without the Holy Spirit, the only thing the church can do with the drug addict and sinners is to reason with them. The drug addict knows he wants drugs. He knows it's wrong. When the drug addict is buying drugs, he knows it is wrong. When he is shooting it into his arms, he knows it's wrong, yet there is an evil spiritual force that drives him. He does not need reason. He needs an anointed person who has the Spirit of the Lord to deliver him from the powers of darkness.

God is shaking the world's foundation. People are coming to the church hungering for God's truth to give them deliverance, salvation, wisdom, and truth. They look to us Christians for spiritual guidance. If we are not spiritually prepared, we will miss harvest opportunities.

In our Christian circles, there is little spiritual knowledge on the actual workings of God's power in our lives (Eph. 3:7). Many Christians do not know how to receive grace for anointing, or where to receive it, or what to do with it. To me, this is the apostasy of the church.

Jesus declared, "And if the blind lead the blind, both shall fall into the ditch" (Matt. 15:14). "For the vile person will speak villainy, and his heart will work iniquity, to practice hypocrisy, and to utter error against the Lord, to make empty the soul of the hungry, and he will cause the drink of the thirsty to fail" (Isa. 32:6).

The ministers of God's Word in the day of Jesus could not understand that Jesus was the Messiah. Their reason stood in the way. Opinions, criticism, and pride are the products of human reason. The only way to understand God's plan for wisdom is through meekness of wisdom (Jas. 3:13). In other words, God's spiritual wisdom is attained through our humility. Yes, there is a wisdom on a higher plane that is only attained by grace through our humility.

The religious leaders did not submit their hearts to meekness by asking God for spiritual understanding of his ways. Instead, they gave themselves to indignation and every foul spirit (Matt. 21:15; Acts 5:17; Rom. 2:8). Jesus, on the other hand, taught them how to be moved by compassion and mercy.

When the Bible talks about hypocrisy, whom does it refer to? It couldn't be sinners because they are doing what is natural to them: sin. It is talking about believers and mainly to ministers. We are the ones who claim to know God and study his Bible. When we don't obey God's Word, yet we claim to be Christians, we are telling the world that we are hypocrites.

Jesus said,

> *Ye hypocrites, well did Isaiah prophesy of you, saying, this people draweth nigh unto me with their mouth, and*

> *honoureth me with their lips; but their heart is far from me. But in vain they do worship me, teaching for doctrines the commandments of men.*
>
> —Matt. 15:8–9

"Hosanna! Hosanna! Hosanna!" they cried when Jesus Christ, the son of God, entered into Jerusalem. A couple of days later they cried out a different tune: "Crucify him! Crucify him! Crucify him!"

What happened? Who turned their hearts around? When they first cried *hosanna* with their lips, their hearts where saying, "We worship you as long as you do what we want. We worship you as long as you do things our way. We worship you as long as you do not ask us to deny ourselves and carry our own cross."

As ministers and Christians, we must yield our inward beings to God or else we are hypocrites. This is how we know people through the spirit. If the same Spirit leads us all, we will all obey the same commandments. Therefore, we will have the same fruits. Jesus rebuked the ministers of his day for not bringing wisdom and righteousness to their inward being. If we listen to the Holy Spirit, he will guide us to all truth. Jesus said in Matthew 23:24–28,

> *Ye blind guides, which strain at a gnat, and swallow a camel. Woe unto you, scribes and Pharisees, hypocrites! For ye make clean the outside of the cup and of the platter, but within they are full of extortion and excess. Thou blind Pharisee, cleanse first that which is within the cup and platter, that the outside of them may be clean also. Woe unto you scribes and Pharisees, hypocrites! For ye are like unto*

> *whited sepulchers, which indeed appear beautiful outward, but are within full of dead men's bones, and of all uncleanness. Even so ye also outwardly appear righteous unto men, but within ye are full of hypocrisy and iniquity.*

People are not fools. They know when something is wrong. In the past, ministers have sinned and brought a reproach to the gospel. They didn't sin because they weren't anointed. They sinned because they failed to lay hold of this one spiritual truth: it is the perfect will of God for everyone to submit his inward being to the obedience of Jesus Christ, one thought at a time (2 Cor. 10:5).

If we ministers are not obeying the Word of God with our inward man, then the resurrected Word, Jesus Christ, will not recognize us when we stand before him. Jesus has foreseen that terrible day and has told us in advance that many ministers will stand before him but he will say, "I never knew you: depart from me ye that work iniquity" (Matt. 7:22–23).

Take your thoughts, your feelings, and your desires and declare with holy anger once and for all in your life, "I will trust the Lord. His Word is final in my life in any situation! I will bring every thought to the obedience of Jesus Christ." Praise God!

Soon, only the Word of God will matter in our lives. The Word of God has become our substance and our food. Let us learn to depend less on our abilities and more on his abilities and promises. Let us realize that we depend on something we cannot see or touch, yet it sustains our lives in perfect harmony. Let us have growing awareness of the invisible arm of God. Let us learn to walk on water until walking on water becomes natural. Praise God!

WALKING EPISTLES

Forasmuch as ye are manifestly declared to be the epistle of Christ ministered by us, written not with ink, but with the Spirit of the living God; not in tables of stone, but in fleshy tables of the heart

—2 Cor. 3:3

When the Holy Spirit came to earth, he came when people were on their knees seeking the promise. When the Spirit came, the apostles began to do greater works than Jesus Christ had done. Before these events took place, Jesus Christ had already prophesied and declared these marvelous things unto them: "And behold, I send the promise of my Father upon you: but tarry ye in the city of Jerusalem, until ye be endued with power from on high" (Luke 24:49).

In the New Testament, the works of the apostles were done through the Holy Spirit. As the Spirit of God was with Jesus, the Spirit of God was with the apostles. Ordinary men touched by the Holy Spirit did extraordinary feats. It was not men who did those things but the Spirit through them. Not human abilities but God in them. They submitted their lives to the Spirit, and God gave them an abundance of grace.

The presence of the Holy Spirit permeated the hearts of the apostles and the ministers of the New Testament. They submitted to the Spirit, and God filled their lives to the point that even their shadows healed the sick. When they put their hands on handkerchiefs, the presence of God filled the cloth. Then they put those handkerchiefs on the sick, and the sickness could not stand against such holy presence.

What has happened to our churches? The church began with great power and demonstration of the Holy Spirit, not with persuasive sermons. Now there is little Holy Spirit power with few demonstrations but plenty of persuasive sermons. The opposite of what is written in the Word has occurred. "And my speech and my preaching was not with enticing words of man's wisdom, but in demonstration of the Spirit and of power: That your faith should not stand in the wisdom of men, but in the power of God" (1 Cor. 2:4–5).

The demonstration of the power of the Holy Spirit was never meant to fade but to increase in the church. The power of God was always meant to flow through yielded vessels to reach the unbeliever. In the heart of God, his things are always meant to increase and not to decrease (Luke 2:52; Acts 6:7; Acts 9:22; Acts 16:5; 1 Cor. 3:6–7; Col. 2:19).

God is a God of abundance. He does not lack anything nor does his power fade. He is the same yesterday, today, and forever (Heb. 13:8). So what has happened? Why did the church lose the anointing of the Holy Spirit? Somebody has to give an account to God. Somebody dropped the ball somewhere along the way.

The church lost the knowledge of how to submit to God with total trust in his power and on his Word. All that has happened, is happening, and will happen has been foretold by God:

> *O foolish Galatians, who hath bewitched you, that ye should not obey the truth, before whose eyes Jesus Christ hath been evidently set forth, crucified among you? Are ye so foolish? Having begun in the Spirit, are ye now made perfect by the flesh? Have ye suffered so many things in vain? If it be yet in vain.*
>
> —Gal. 3:1–4

The church began in the Spirit with great power. Then the church reasoned the power out of God's Word and brought the things of God to the natural level. However, the anointing cannot be brought lower. The anointing stayed at the higher level that is only attained through obedience to his Word. Without knowledge of spiritual things, the church will always take the route of logic and reason. This is the natural path. However, the supernatural is where God intended for his church to live.

Throughout time, man has always tried to control the Holy Spirit instead of submitting to him. In the very beginning, man tried to buy the Spirit, so he could manipulate the Spirit for his own profit:

And when Simeon saw that through laying on of the apostle's hands the Holy Ghost was given, he offered them money, Saying, give me also this power. . . . But Peter said unto him, thy money perish with thee, because thou hast thought that the gift of God may be purchased with money . . . thy heart is not right in the sight of God. Repent therefore of this thy wickedness, and pray God, perhaps the thought of thine heart may be forgiven thee. For I perceive that thou art in the gall of bitterness, and in the bond of iniquity.

—Acts 8:18–23

Peter told Simeon that Simeon's heart was not right in the eyes of God. Our focus should be on our hearts. David prayed, "Create in me a clean heart, O God; and renew a right spirit within me" (Ps. 51:10). Let's look at our hearts and submit ourselves to God. Our hearts are the vessels of God. However, if our hearts are full of wrong attitudes, we need to bring them before God. We need to allow God to fill our hearts with all that is pleasing to him.

The church has come to another spiritual crossroad as Israel did in the days of Moses and Joshua. Will we enter into the Promised Land to take the promises by faith and with spiritual force and knowledge? Or are we going to murmur against God and hide behind our reason in cowardice and blindness?

God is raising up a new generation of believers who will acknowledge the Word of God over the natural and enter into the promise. A courageous generation who are willing to step out of the boat and believe God's promises. A wise generation is coming forth, full of the knowledge of God that has been handed to them from generation to generation. A new day has begun. On the horizon, we see a change in hearts, attitudes, and viewpoints.

Has God begun to stir up his five-fold ministers to again teach the ways of the Holy Spirit? Yes, he has. The wind has begun to blow again. Power and wisdom is returning to the church. The latter rain has begun. The world is about to experience great power and demonstration of the Spirit by not a few but by congregations and churches. Why? Because this is God's church, not man's church. God is a jealous God.

How can the Holy Spirit fill us, so we can find fulfillment in our personal lives, win souls to the kingdom of heaven, and advance the kingdom of God? How can we go about in the power of the Holy Spirit—as Jesus did—to accomplish greater works in the Spirit? How can this awesome knowledge become a reality in our lives? "How God anointed Jesus of Nazareth with the Holy Ghost and with power: who went about doing good, and healing all that were oppressed of the Devil; for God was with him" (Acts 10:38).

In John 3:34, we read that the Spirit was upon Jesus without measure. Can the Holy Spirit also be upon us in that way? The Bible does not forbid us to have the Spirit without measure. A matter of fact, Jesus said we would do greater works than he. If we are called to do greater works than he, it is because we can also have the Spirit of God upon us without measure. "Verily, verily, I say unto you, he that believeth on me, the works that I do shall he do also; and greater works than these shall he do; because I go unto my Father" (John 14:12).

If God gave us his Son as the sacrificial lamb and did not keep his own Son from us, will he not also give us all good things (Rom. 8:32)? Jesus said, "If ye then, being evil, know how to give good gifts unto your children, how much more shall your Father which is in heaven give good things to them that ask him?" (Matt. 7:11).

Jesus taught that greater works than the ones he performed through the Spirit will be done through those who believe in him because he went to the Father. Now, these greater works are works that make man marvel (John 5:20). Every time Jesus did something supernatural, the people marveled and praised God. This is our goal. Doing miracles is a simple thing for God, but he must receive all the glory. Therefore, it is man who needs to be tried and tested so that man will not exalt himself with pride.

After the resurrection, Jesus went to the Father. He did not arrive before the Father empty handed. Jesus arrived glorified: "But this spake he of the Spirit, which they that believe on him should receive: for the Holy Ghost was not yet given; because that Jesus was not yet glorified" (John 7:39).

Before Jesus could be glorified, he first had to humble himself, suffer, and shed his blood for us on the cross. After the third day, Jesus rose from the grave with glory. He came to the Father and kicked the accuser of the brethren (the Devil) out from the presence of the Father. Jesus agreed with the Father that his blood washes all our sins away.

Jesus came before the Father victorious over life and death. Whenever we pray in the name of Jesus Christ, the Son and the Father stand in union in heaven to bring about whatever we ask. Once the Father and Son unite in agreement, the Holy Spirit moves with power. Because of this threefold union, we will do greater works.

> *And whatsoever ye shall ask in my name, that will I do, that the Father may be glorified in the Son. If ye shall ask any thing in my name, I will do it. . . . And I will pray the Father, and he shall give you another Comforter, that he may abide with you forever. . . . At that day ye shall know that I am in my Father, and ye in me, and I in you . . . He that hath my commandments, and keepeth them, he it is that loveth me: and he that loveth me shall be loved of my Father, and I will love him, and will manifest myself to him.*
>
> —John 14

Since Jesus has been glorified, the Holy Spirit has access to our hearts. In the Old Testament, the Holy Spirit had limited access to people through the blood of animals. Now, he has complete access to us through the blood of Jesus Christ. Because of this, the apostles could be full of the Holy Spirit (Acts 4:8; 6:3; 11:24).

"It is finished," Jesus cried and then died on the cross. I can write an entire book on this one phrase and still not capture the immensity of his work on the cross. For the moment, we know that Jesus completed his work and sat down next to the Father. It is our responsibility to bring all obedience to God. It is our job to stop conforming to the present world but to be transformed by the renewing of our minds. We must stop offering God excuses, self-justifications, and reasons why we do not obey his Word. Instead we should simply obey.

For thousand of years, God has heard all types of excuses. A generation is coming forth who will not make excuses. They will completely obey through a contrite heart. Destiny and the latter rain are upon us.

John the Baptist testified that he saw the Holy Spirit descend on Jesus as a dove. A dove represents a gentle creature that is sensitive to the things around him. A dove lands on places where he finds safety, security, and acceptance. When a dove senses danger or discomfort, he simply flies away. This speaks of Jesus' personality.

This dove remained on Jesus (John 1:32). What made the Holy Spirit remain with Jesus? Jesus Christ's willingness to submit to his leading. Jesus said, "The flesh is weak, but the spirit is willing." Jesus always followed the leading of the Spirit, even to death.

The Holy Spirit will always lead us to do the will of the Father and to glorify Jesus. Jesus lived his life by saying, "Not my will but your will be done." He always did the will of the Father.

The moment we kneel down as Jesus did in Gethsemane and pray for every situation in our lives, "Not my will but your will be done," the Father will see us as his son and will send his Holy Spirit upon us. When we carry our cross and deny ourselves, this pleases the Father. When we die to ourselves, the Holy Spirit will resurrect us unto newness of life as he did Jesus Christ.

I know that there have been times when the Spirit of God touched our hearts, but that feeling or anointing went away. That happened because the Spirit will only remain on us until we begin to do our own will. Here is the problem: the Holy Spirit is sensitive to us. We must also be sensitive to him and understand what pleases him so that he can continually stay upon us.

This is God's greatest challenge to man. The purpose of man is to obey God's commandments. Yet, we cannot obey without grace and the Spirit. So, the only thing we can do is submit. Devils, demons, or seducing spirits cannot submit because they are perverted and damned beings. They work all types of perversion and iniquity among people. If you find it within yourself to continually submit your soul to God, you have conquered legions of devils and the forces of darkness.

The Word of God says that Jesus was full of grace and truth (John 1:14). Are you full of grace and truth? If not, what are you full of? More importantly, why are you full of this?

> *Being filled with all unrighteousness, fornication, wickedness, covetousness, maliciousness; full of envy, murder, debate, deceit, malignity; whisperers, backbiters, haters of God, despiteful, proud, boasters, inventors of evil things, disobedient to parents, without understanding, covenant breakers, without natural affection, implacable, unmerciful.*
>
> —Rom. 1:29–31

You are caught in a spiritual war. You are being deceived, and this is not a game or a joke. If you don't wake up in time, you will live in your worst nightmare. There will be no waking up because your time is over. Now is the time of faith, hope, and grace.

In hell, there is no more hope but eternal screams of horror and torment. Understand this, you will always be a conscious being. You will never die. You will never stop existing. You are like God in that you are immortal. You must choose where to spend eternity. One day you will stand before God to give an account of your choices. As a minister of God, I am preaching the truth to you.

Wouldn't you rather humble yourself before God, so you can be full of truth and grace?

> *Now the God of hope fill you with all joy and peace in believing, that ye may abound in hope through the power of the Holy Ghost. And I myself also am persuaded of you, my brethren, that ye also are full of goodness, filled with all knowledge, able also to admonish one another.*
>
> —Rom. 15:13–14

Your heart is like a cup that holds spiritual things—thoughts and emotions. Stop and meditate. Ask yourself why you feel the way you do. Where did these feelings come from? Feelings are spiritual things that will lead you and control your life if you submit to them. Whatever you submit to will govern your heart and will rule over you, whether it be bitterness, hate, jealousy, and lust, or if you submit to love—joy and peace. "But be filled with the Spirit" (Eph. 5:18).

God has desired to dwell in the hearts of his people. Before God's glory can come in, he must first clean the vessel by the washing of the Word (Eph. 5:26). We are vessels called to hold God's Spirit. The Spirit comes upon us but also wants to remain in us. If we resist the working of God in our lives, we will be vessels full of ourselves and not of his Spirit. "But we have this treasure in earthen vessels, that the excellency of the power may be of God, and not of us" (2 Cor. 4:7).

Stop resisting the working of God in your life. Stop murmuring against people and circumstances, and allow God to use them to work in your life. The more evil comes before you, the more of God's grace will rest upon you. Learn to be sensitive to the Spirit and submit to the Spirit. Do not allow pride to deceive you. Do not allow Satan to deceive you through fleshly power. Always use the power that God grants you to do good and to edify your brother.

God wants to endue us with power. He gives his power a little at a time. He gives anointing and wisdom, then sees how the Christian handles such privilege. If the Devil deceives a person through pride, God will not give more power to that person. If he conquers the lies of the Devil and continues to submit, God will give him still more power.

Satan so easily deceives us into believing that we are better than others. God may take us into a higher level, and there Satan will whisper to our hearts, "Everyone is wrong except you." Weakness in ourselves attracts more of God's power into our lives and not pride. This attitude of humility allows us to continue with the Spirit into higher levels in Christ. Therefore, learn to have attitudes that are pleasing to him and say, "I am wrong, and everybody else is right." As you submit your thoughts to God you will learn to discern wisdom and the perfect will of God. Not all criticism from others is of God. Even so, when criticism comes, you will not be offended. Instead, you will find that small pearl of truth within that criticism and apply it to your life. You will continue to grow, mature, and transform into the image of Christ.

The Bible speaks of two types of vessels. One vessel holds God's glory. The other holds his wrath.

> *Hath not the potter power over the clay, of the same lump to make one vessel unto honour, and another unto dishonour? What if God, willing to shew his wrath, and to make his power known, endured with much longsuffering the vessels of wrath fitted to destruction: and that he might make known the riches of his glory on the vessels of mercy, which he had afore prepared unto glory.*
>
> —Rom. 9:21–23

Now, I ask you, Dear Reader, what type of vessel do you want to be?

For those who study the Bible, I know the above passage refers to Israel and the Gentiles. Nevertheless, it is still true for those who allow God to work in their lives and those who resist God.

> *But in a great house there are not only vessels of gold and silver, but also of wood and of earth; and some to honour, and some to dishonour. If a man therefore purge himself from these, he shall be a vessel unto honour, sanctified, and meet for the master's use, and prepared unto every good work.*
>
> —2 Tim. 2:20–21

God puts the responsibility on us to purge ourselves. How do we purge ourselves? By bringing one thought at a time captive to the obedience of Jesus Christ. "For this is the will of God, even your sanctification, that ye should abstain from fornication: That every one of you should know how to possess his vessel in sanctification and honour" (1 Thess.

4:3–4). Do you know how to possess your vessel now? One thought at a time.

There is power from God to perform the act of bringing into captivity every thought that we may be holy vessels, meet for the Master's use. "For God, who commanded the light to shine out of darkness, hath shined in our hearts, to give the light of the knowledge of the glory of God in the face of Jesus Christ" (2 Cor. 4:6).

People live with no power. Their emotions and their thoughts rule over them because they submit to them. Yet, power is available from God to bring everything in us to his feet. This is what the power of God is for! Obedience to God's Word and submission to the Spirit takes supernatural power. An individual will never change or be transformed unless he finds the grace of God to bring one thought at a time to the feet of Jesus Christ.

In the Old Testament, God showed Israel the importance of washing their bodies and cleansing the inside of cooking vessels (Mark 7:8). However, Israel never understood the spiritual meaning behind these teachings. Water always symbolizes cleaning. How can a person clean something without water? That is why John baptized people in water for repentance. That is why Jesus said in order to enter the kingdom of heaven you must be born of water and the Spirit (John 3:5).

The Word of God is compared to water: "That he might sanctify and cleanse it with the washing of water by the Word, that he might present it to himself a glorious church, not having spot, or wrinkle, or any such thing; but that it should be holy and without blemish" (Eph. 5:27). When you obey the Word of God, it washes you. This symbolizes what happens when you bring your thoughts captive to the obedience of Jesus Christ. This process washes you and transforms you by renewing your mind one thought at a time (Rom. 12:2).

When we submit to the Word of God and obey it rather than our reason, we allow God to constantly deal with our character and our attitudes. If God has access to our inmost being, he will have complete access to our entire life. It is wiser to place your life in God's hand than in your own hands. Believe it or not, when God deals with your heart, it is only for your own benefit.

The moment we stop submitting our souls to God, we turn from God's righteousness to our own righteousness. Our own righteousness is not enough to please God. Submission is always God's plan. Our hearts need to be tried and broken over and over again.

Do you want to experience the presence of God? Do you want the power and anointing of God to grow in your life? When someone does something to irritate you or offend you and anger rises within you, you make a decision. You can either give in to your anger or submit your anger to God. When you submit your anger to God, you will be broken, but the presence of God will overwhelm you. Soon, your life will change. Peace and wisdom will come into your life and the presence of God will follow you.

Do not trust in yourself. Submit to God. His Word will break you, but it will also heal you. Your flesh may rebel against discipline, but your spirit is willing to grow and know God in a deeper relationship. David said, "Heal the bones that you have broken" (Ps. 51:8). A shepherd, David knew what it was to take a wild, untamed lamb and break his legs on purpose, then mend the broken bones and carry that lamb on his shoulders until those wounds healed.

After this incident, the lamb would learn to appreciate the wisdom and the love of the shepherd. The lamb would never again wander away from the good shepherd because there was now a bond of trust, comfort, and love. Jesus said, "I am the good shepherd, and know my sheep, and am known of mine" (John 10:14).

A challenge of God to be transformed into his image

What would it be like to be in the presence of the prophets of God of the Old Testament? When Samuel came into town, the elders trembled at his presence and asked if he came in peace (1 Sam. 16:4). What would it be like to stand before anointed men who knew God and understood his perfect plan for humanity? It must have been a sight to behold John the Baptist cry, "Repent for the kingdom of God is at hand!"

Such men had no time for games. They were men of purpose and because they understood the depths of God, they were ministers of fire. If they were alive today, could the church handle such confrontations from men who beheld such glory of God?

Imagine one of those men being alive today. I believe they would have popped our world. They could have said the following: Is the Word of God true or not? Answer this question once and for all in your life. I am not talking about mentally saying yes until you are blue in the face. I am talking about trusting your entire life to the promises of God and not flinching when the waves and wind hit you.

You tiptoe around God's Word. You know it's God's Word, yet something keeps you from depending totally on it when all the universe is sustained by that same Word. Is this because of caution or reason or common sense? It shows a lack of confidence in your relationship with God's Spirit. Today's the day to turn this around.

Do you want to walk with God's Spirit and walk in the supernatural? Nevertheless, you are too chicken to get out of the boat and take even a couple of steps. You live in the boat while God's spiritual world is floating on top of the water. You know God exists, but reason keeps you from walking on the water. You talk about how great God is in making the boat and all creation, but you do not trust him with your life.

You just conform to the present age when you are supposed to be renewing your mind! Have you reached the point where you want to experience the reality of God more than anything else? Would you do anything that God asks you just to behold God's mighty power? Are you there yet?

Pick up your cross and conquer your murmurings. Love your neighbor and your enemies? Stand your ground believing God's promises to the very end? Completely submit your life to obey God? Even if everything within you screams to disobey God's Word, yet you stand your ground? Even if all the demons in hell come against to disobey God's Word, you endure! Bible men are made of this. The world is not worthy of such men (Heb. 11).

Walking on water is not for spineless people! It is only for Christians—children of God.

I see it over and over again. I try to edify people by telling them of the power of God, yet something stops them from being edified. There's always some doubt, some fear, some reason that allows them to reject the Word. Although I try to edify them, they fight for some point of view or to protect their lifestyle, their flesh, and their sin.

It has nothing to do with my being right and your being wrong. I am talking about knowing the power of God—not just mentally saying that you agree that God is omnipotent but experiencing the power of God in your life. Submit to God, and you will experience the power of God over sin. Afterwards, you will look back and say, "I can't believe that a small devil like lust kept me bound for so many years. Thank you, Lord Jesus, for delivering me!"

When preachers preach that God delivers, everybody says *amen*. However, when I, being a teacher of God's Word, explain it step by step, all hell breaks loose. When preachers shout that God is able to do everything and that nothing is impossible for him, the congregation goes wild with applause. However, when I teach that Christians need to completely submit and depend on God's Word in order to come out of the boat because God's Word is able to uphold them, then all the demons in hell come against me.

I must conclude that we earthly minded humans like to stay in the comfort of the boat and only give mental agreement that God is able to sustain us on top of the water. When a teacher dares us to step out of the boat and out of our comfort zone, we resist.

That is how most Christians live. They say, "Yes, God is mighty. Yes, God is all powerful." Yet, they do not believe and stand on one promise of God's Word. They will never know personally that God is able to uphold all those who stand on his Word. This is like the time of Moses when the people beheld God from afar because they were afraid of him. They asked Moses to climb the mountain and seek God while they waited on the bottom. Many Christians want preachers and teachers to talk about how great God is, but they do not want their boat to be rocked.

There is also another attitude in our churches. Christians are waiting for God's power to supernaturally come down from heaven, pick them up with lovingkindness, and carry them across the water. No! That attitude does not move God. That attitude does not make Jesus stand up from his throne and applaud us, like he did Stephen (Acts 7:56). God wants us to believe on his Word and step out of the boat with no strings attached, just raw faith in God's Word.

While Jesus Christ hung on the cross on Calvary, people ridiculed him saying that if he was the son of God, to come down from the cross (Matt. 27:39–44). For many people, Jesus dying on the cross for their sins was not enough.

Jesus Christ already died for our sorrow and pain. People walk around this world in so much self-pity for what they have suffered. They are waiting for that sorrow to magically lift from their lives. They want God to take away all the pain, not knowing that they have to submit their sorrow and pain to him. They do not want to submit. They want Christ to come down from his throne and surgically remove it.

Many Christians cry to God, "Give me more power, anointing, patience, love, faith, etc. Give me. Give me. Give me. Do it for me. Make me feel better. Dying on the cross for me is not good enough. Come down from the cross and show me that you are God!" God is not a magical genie who obeys our wishes. We must learn the secret of how to submit. We must learn his ways.

God puts us in a natural world and puts his Word in a supernatural world. He dares his creation to step out and believe on his Word in the face of the wind and waves. Whoever does this has God's attention. Don't bother telling me about your point of view. You either know God's power or all you have is a head full of information called religion or imaginations. The boat you are protecting is where I came from. I already know everything about your boat. Besides, I have news for you, your boat has sprung a leak, and it is sinking.

I come to you again. Is God real? Is the Word of God true? Or is everything one big fairy tale? Don't say God's Word is real and act as if it were a fairy tale. The moment your heart agrees that it is real, you'll begin to step out of the boat into God's world where everything is possible, where God's power never runs dry.

God's Word will never change. What has to change is you and your attitudes. So far, you know what it is to have church inside the boat—wonderful songs, persuasive sermons, and a lot of emotion or intellect—while the real church is out there floating on the water where men see and stand in awe.

We haven't even scratched the surface to understand who we are in Christ Jesus. You haven't even begun to understand the image of God in which you are made. You haven't begun to understand the depths of the breath that

God blew into man. You have no idea what the Holy Spirit inside of you is capable of accomplishing. You have no idea how real the spiritual world is. You have no idea how powerful the Word of God is. You haven't taken your first step on water.

Jesus Christ said to Peter, "Come," and there was more authority and power in that one word than any power you can imagine. One word of the Creator and all the physical laws of the creation obey. Now, he has challenged mankind to believe in his Word and to depend on the Word. Come out of the boat and walk, not on your strength but in God's unseen power.

God manifested in the flesh is Jesus Christ. Everything happened as he said because there is no lie in him. He told Peter, "Come," and Peter walked on water. He told Lazarus, "Come forth," and Lazarus arose from the dead. He told the storm, "Be still," and the storm subsided. He told demons and sickness, "Come out," and people were made whole. Nothing can resist his words. All he asks is that you believe in his Word. He has all power to sustain his Word.

The New Testament is filled with promises:

I can do all things through Christ which strengthens me.

—Phil. 4:13

My God shall supply all your need according to his riches in glory by Christ Jesus.

—Phil. 4:19

By his stripes we were healed.

—1 Pet. 2:24

Greater is he that is within me than he that is in the world.

—1 John 4:4

As you begin to walk and depend on the Word of God, you will no longer be an ordinary man because God's Spirit will be upon you.

"For we walk by faith and not by sight" (2 Cor. 5:7). The world walks by sight and reacts to what they see. We do not react to what we see. We react to what we believe, and we believe that the Word of God has more authority than what we see. We are no longer victims of our limited sight. Before, bad news brought despair. Now, when we get bad news we rejoice, for we are about to see a supernatural moving of God in our lives. Who knows how God will gain the victory, but if God orchestrated this universe then God can bring us out of any dilemma.

People live their lives reacting to situations with reason instead of with obedience, then they wonder why God doesn't bless them. Commit your life to God, and let the Word of God be final in any situation. Let the Word of God map out your life.

Trust God as a child trusts his father. Don't wonder if God misunderstands you. He made you. He hears all your thoughts and knows the secrets of your heart. If God has the wisdom and power to hold the universe in the palm of his hand, do you think he can't take care of you?

Your perception of reality is formed in your mind. When you look out your window, what do you see? When you look out to the horizon, what do you see? When you look at a bird fly and a fish swim so naturally, what do you see?

When you look at the beauty of a flower, what do you see? When you look up to the sky, what do you see? When you look into your child's eyes, what do you see? Everywhere I look, I see the hand of God. Everything is a miracle.

Are you a Christian who believes that God created everything by his word and sustains everything by his Word, and yet you don't stand on even one promise (Heb. 1:3)? How pathetic is that? You'd rather gripe and complain than believe that all things work for good to those that love him (Rom. 8:28)?

You have to love adventure if you want to step out of the boat. Let the new generation of young people enter into the promises of God. This message is for those who want to walk in the supernatural things of God and are tired of dead religion.

How far can our faith reach? As far as God reveals it to our hearts day by day. Faith has no limit or boundaries except the ones we set up. I don't know about you, but I'm confident that God is able to perform his Word, and he is not a respecter of persons. He is just waiting for people to believe in his Word and step out of the boat.

In God's eyes, he has already made us to sit in heavenly places with his Son, Jesus Christ (Eph. 2:6). The only thing is, we do not fully understand that yet. We do not have to wait for death to experience all of God because in heavenly places there is no time but an ever-present now, an eternal now. "Now, faith is . . ." (Heb. 11:1).

If you can see yourself as God sees you, this world will become your playground. Nothing will be too big to overcome, since the physical was made from faith and is governed by faith (Heb. 11). So our birthright in Christ Jesus is to grow in faith and take hold of all our inheritance in Christ.

If Christ Jesus sits in the heavenly with every power and authority under his feet, then it is also under our feet, for we are in Christ Jesus. If you are not in Christ Jesus, this book teaches you exactly how to be in Christ Jesus.

You may say, "I do not know what reality is." We all choose are own reality. The world's reality is temporal, but our reality is eternal. The world's reality is their sight; our reality is the Word of God. The world's reality is sin; our reality is freedom in Christ Jesus.

My old, temporal reality has been swallowed up by the presence of God. It has been confronted by the Word of God. The moment I accepted Jesus Christ as my Lord and Savior, I am no longer of the temporal but of the eternal kingdom of God, the new birth in me. Whose gospel will you choose to obey? Jesus came to be your light and show you the true reality.

> *As is the earthy, such are they also that are earthy: and as is the heavenly, such are they also that are heavenly. And as we have born the image of the earthy, we shall also bear the image of the heavenly.*
>
> —1 Cor. 15:48–49

> *He that is unjust, let him be unjust still: and he which is filthy, let him be filthy still: and he that is righteous, let him be righteous still: and he that is holy, let him be holy still. And behold, I come quickly; and my reward is with me, to give every man according as his work shall be.*
>
> —Rev. 22:11–12

Come on, Beloved. Stop reasoning, and come out of the boat. Are you going to settle on existing in the tiny boat and not experience the vast ocean? Are you going to acknowledge that God is God only with your mind and never believe it with your heart? Don't wait until you are dead and stand before God and then look back and wish you'd stepped out of the boat. Don't wait until you're old and dying and then beg God for the second chance to step out of the boat in your life. Your time is now. Your time is here. Get out of the boat. Get out of the boat and walk in the Spirit with power and wisdom.

"Ye are of God, little children, and have overcome them: because greater is he that is in you, than he that is in the world" (1 John 4:4). Don't let this beautiful, eternal verse simply be another religious saying. But, let this verse be a reality in your life. As you bring your thoughts to his feet, his presence will come into your life. If his presence is in your life, that presence is greater than any other presence; greater than sickness and seducing devils, fear, or depression; greater than anger and violence. Live with the reality of the promises of God.

The world depends upon your coming out of the boat and showing them the power of God. Our God depends upon your being a yielded vessel. Christian's lives are sometimes the only Bible others will ever read. If they see in you a tormented soul just like themselves, they do not need your weak god. But if they see a soul submitted to God, with the power, wisdom, and Spirit of God resting upon you, they will want to know about your God.

Walking Epistles

Ye are our epistle written in our hearts, known and read of all men.

—2 Cor. 3:2

Chapter 9

WALKING INTO SPIRITUAL WARFARE

> *He teacheth my hands to war, so that a bow of steel is broken by mine arms. Thou hast also given me the shield of thy salvation: and thy right hand hath holden me up, and thy gentleness hath made me great . . . I have pursued mine enemies, and overtaken them: neither did I turn again till they were consumed.*
>
> —Ps. 18:34–35,37

The church has entered into times of violence, not physical violence but a spiritual violence. The church is eagerly waiting for a new anointing of Holy Spirit power. The old anointing and yesterday's wineskin have been used up. A fresh anointing and a new wineskin with fresh wine are in the earth. A change of guards in heavenly places is taking place.

The church wants to press forward but has no knowledge. You are called to lead the church into this new era.

God is calling you, Dear Reader. You now have more understanding of God's ways than many Christians.

Answer the call of God, and go to Bible school. Although, Bible school cannot teach you how to love your enemy, it will teach you other aspects of the ministry that are vitally important. What Bible schools cannot teach, the Holy Spirit will. There are spiritual things that only God can teach you.

God can use you. Begin to seek him. Everything is coming together. The ways of God are being revealed, and everything is now making sense.

> *And he gave some, apostles; some prophets; evangelists, pastors, and teachers, for the perfecting of the saints, for the work of the ministry, for the edifying of the body of Christ. . . . That we henceforth be no more children tossed to and fro, and carried about with every wind of doctrine, by the sleight of men, and cunning craftiness, whereby they lie in wait to deceive.*
>
> —Eph. 4:11,14

> *And from the days of John the Baptist until now the kingdom of heaven suffereth violence and the violent take it by force.*
>
> —Matt. 11:12

A new and profound understanding of violence has come forth into the land. The things of God, My Precious Reader, will not drop into your lap. They demand your violence. However, violence without wisdom does not profit. Once you receive knowledge, it is up to you to apply it. It is up to you to walk in it, and after you walk in it, God will give you more wisdom to answer the rest of your questions.

> *I therefore so run, not as uncertainly; so fight I, not as one that beateth the air: But I keep under my body and bring it into subjection: lest that by any means, when I have preached to others, I myself should be a castaway.*
>
> —1 Cor. 9:26–27

There are two types of violence: physical and spiritual. Physical violence only seeks to protect your rights in this physical world. Truth will always remain, and after all has been said and done, whatever you fought for in this physical world will eventually pass away. Anything done in the physical by the physical is only vanity and temporal.

Spiritual violence seeks your eternal rights. As you can see, the spiritual has more importance than anything physical. Spiritual violence will give way to faith and humility. These attitudes will draw the grace of God into our lives. With the grace of God, we will live in the world of God where all things are possible to them who believe. With the grace of God, the meek shall ask for whatsoever, and God will give it to them.

The only real control we have is control of our attitudes and actions. We control how we live and what we produce. We cannot control others. We cannot change others, but we can decide to give our own lives and thoughts over to God. Therefore, our focus should not be on others but on ourselves. The day is coming when we will all stand before God and give an account of our own lives, not the lives of others.

Physical violence obeys the voice of reason. Hurting, revenge, cynicism, sarcasm, criticism, and frustration are the constant companions of violent people. With time these will damage one's relationships. This is the way of the Devil.

Spiritual violence is violence that can be found within us. It can be used against our own souls. We need spiritual violence to bring all our being into submission to God. We cannot humble ourselves before God without first being spiritually violent within ourselves.

Physical violence prefers to hurt everyone else and be self-protecting. Spiritual violence prefers to be offended rather than offend. Therefore, understand the ways of God and prefer to be accused than to accuse, prefer to be judged than to judge, prefer to be mocked than to mock, prefer to be oppressed than to oppress, prefer to be wounded than to wound, prefer to have the presence of God rather than be resisted by God.

Make no mistake, Dear Reader, you are in a spiritual battle. Life is a battle. You are fighting for your eternity and your anointing. God is in the business of saving souls twenty-four hours a day, seven days a week. Satan is in the business of deceiving souls twenty-four hours a day, seven days a week. You are caught right in the middle. If you do not join God in the battle over your soul, there will be no victory for you, no reward of the spoils of war. If you are not fighting against your soul, then you are a prisoner of your soul. The Devil has deceived you.

The Enemy has set a trap for you. Spiritual knowledge allows you to understand where you are. Spiritual violence will allow you to come out of that snare. The Devil has centuries of experience. You are dealing with a cunning liar who knows exactly which buttons to push in your life. He is the god of this world. Do not underestimate him. He is always at war against you and commands a highly skilled and disciplined army of demons for the sole purpose of deceiving you.

> *. . . lest he fall into reproach and the snare of the devil.*
>
> —1 Tim. 3:7

> *But they that will be rich fall into temptation and a snare, and into many foolish and hurtful lusts, which drown men in destruction and perdition.*
>
> —1 Tim. 6:9

> *In meekness instructing those that oppose themselves; if God peradventure will give them repentance to the acknowledging of the truth; and that they may recover themselves out of the snare of the devil, who are taken captive by him at his will.*
>
> —2 Tim. 2:25–26

> *For as a snare shall it come on all them that dwell on the face of the whole earth. Watch ye therefore, and pray always, that ye may be accounted worthy to escape all these things that shall come to pass, and to stand before the Son of man.*
>
> —Luke 21:35–36

I am a warrior for God. I carry my cross, since the moment I awake. If have no pity on myself. I am called to train you in the ways of God. I believe you are tired of being deceived by the Devil. I know you are tired of being a spectator, watching your life go by or watching others enjoy their dreams and goals. I know that you go to work and sometimes wonder if there is more to life than just making money and making ends meet. Yes, there is something else. You are called to be a warrior for God, to experience God in your life and fulfill his call.

Are you ready for war? Are you ready for your spiritual drill sergeant? I will take you by the hand and teach you about your enemy, your weapons, and drill you. Are you ready to begin boot camp?

War separates the boys from the men. Spiritual warfare separates average Christians from mature Christians. A warrior must know his weapons, his battleground, and, most importantly, his enemy. Knowledge of spiritual things is important. *If for some reason you are frustrated in your walk with God, understand that there is a spiritual truth you have not attained. You must reach forward and press toward the mark* (Phil. 3:13–14).

In Joshua's generation, their war was twofold. Ours is only onefold. They had to fight both a physical and a spiritual war. When they destroyed a city, they could not covet anything. This dealt with the heart of the people. Once you deal with things of the heart, you are dealing with spiritual matters. In Joshua's day, those who took anything from the enemy were destroyed by God because of disobedience (Josh. 7:20–26).

Today, our war is spiritual and not physical. Please understand this one concept. No violence is done in the physical, only inside our beings. "For we wrestle not against flesh and blood, but against principalities, against powers, against rulers of the darkness of this world, against spiritual wickedness in high places" (Eph. 6:12).

These principalities, powers, rulers of darkness, and spiritual wickedness in high places do not and cannot submit to the Word of God. They are perverted, damned beings who will cause men to rebel against God. That is why it is so hard for individuals to submit to authority. It takes power from the Holy Spirit to obey God and submit to his Word. The moment an individual is enlightened to submit to the Word of God, he will have to fight all the powers of hell to submit a single thought to God. However, the grace of God is sufficient to accomplish this task.

God dealt with the people of Israel through physical means that they might understand the spiritual significance. Unfortunately, they never were able to grasp those spiritual truths. Now, it is up to us to grasp these spiritual truths, to run with them, and press forward into the promises of God.

God had promised the land of Canaan by a covenant to Abraham and his descendants. Now Joshua was ready to lead Israel into the land of Canaan, take it, and enter into the Promised Land. Until that moment, the people of Israel had only a promise, a legacy of miracles handed over to them from generation to generation. However, God was not about to hand them the Promised Land on a silver platter. They had to believe God for the promises and fight for them. Only through violence and faith were they allowed to enter the Promised Land (Josh. 1:1,2).

The word *possess* implies a violent takeover (Josh. 1:11). The only reason Joshua's generation passed over the Jordan River was to confront a fortified city in faith and obedience to God's Word. They took up arms and prepared their hearts for war, even if the enemy was stronger, even if the enemy had fortified himself behind strong walls. God said that the land was theirs, so they arose and took it by a violent faith. When God saw that they dared to believe his Word, the power of God sent the walls of Jericho crashing down.

The oldest city ever excavated is the city of Jericho with its walls broken down, a testimony to all that God is able to perform miracles through people who are not afraid to believe and stand on his Word. If people are willing to step out of the boat of fear, reason, and self-justification and trust in his Word, they will behold God's power.

God has said that sin shall not have dominion over you (Rom. 6:14). Are you going to stand around with all the other carnal wimps and give God the same excuses that generation after generation have given him? God is tired of fleshy excuses. How long will you tolerate sin in your thinking? Stand up and fight. Take possession of this promise.

There is opposition from demonic forces when ministers preach about holiness and how to wash our hands before the Lord (Jas. 4:8; Rom. 6:22). These demonic forces want to continually govern people's lives through sin. They do not want people to be set free by the power of God's truth. They do not want Christians to become victorious but to be wishy-washy in their faith. The Devil wants people to be as dogs that continually return to their vomit or as swines that return to the mud after being washed (2 Pet. 2:22).

Demonic forces know that if Christians focus on submitting their souls to Christ, they will enter into a new relationship with God. Devils know that this draws greater anointing and grace into Christians' lives. Demons know that greater anointing will break the yoke of bondage in their personal lives, then in their families, then in their churches, then in their communities. Demons know they cannot stand in the presence of such anointing, so they will have to flee and relinquish their seat of power.

When God told Joshua to prepare the people for battle, Joshua did not complain or resist God. He obeyed God. Have you ever asked yourself why it is so hard to obey the Word of God? It is simple, because the forces of evil are fighting you. These rulers of darkness keep people blind to the glorious light of the gospel. They want people to remain in the realm of emotions and intellect and never venture to a higher spiritual level.

Joshua was one of the original twelve spies of the land of Canaan. He and Caleb brought back a good report while the other ten said the Israelites could not overtake the inhabitants of the land. The people of Israel cried and murmured against God. They wanted to stone Joshua and Caleb.

Do you think God approves of murmuring? People who murmur against everything negative that comes into their lives do not understand spiritual truths. They do not understand how to rest from their works and allow God to work in their character. They do not trust in the wisdom of God to wait for the salvation of the Lord. They have no anointing or grace to submit their soul to the cross. They constantly resist God instead of allowing circumstances to be an opportunity to obey God. They want to walk their own way, understand their own truth, and find their own life.

God said,

> *How long shall I bear with this evil congregation which murmur against me? I have heard the murmurings of the children of Israel, which they murmur against me . . . your carcasses shall fall in this wilderness . . . I the Lord have said, I will surely do it unto all this evil congregation, that are gathered together against me: in this wilderness they shall be consumed, and there they shall die.*
>
> —Num. 14:27–35

Do you think God takes eternal life lightly? Do you think God is kidding around with his commandments? No, you are the only one that is playing around. "When I was a child, I spake as a child, I understood as a child, I thought as a child: but when I became a man, I put away childish things" (1 Cor. 13:11).

Joshua had to fulfill his destiny in his generation. The children of Israel decided to obey God and arm themselves with courage and a violent faith. Joshua began to prepare the mighty men of valor (Josh. 1:14). "And they utterly destroyed all that was in the city, both man and woman, young and old, and ox, and sheep, and ass, with the edge of the sword" (Josh. 6:21).

Are you ready to utterly destroy sin in your life? Are you ready to bring every thought captive to the feet of Jesus Christ? Or do you want to keep some of the enemies' belongings? Sorry, no spoils from the enemy. You are either a new creature in Christ Jesus in the process of renewing or simply a deformed Christian who refuses to submit to the washing of the Word.

War is brutal, savage, and violent beyond what we can imagine. We do not completely grasp the essence of what war is like. There is a difference between reading about war and being in one. There is only one rule in hand-to-hand combat and that is to kill or be killed.

The spiritual war that God has called us to is a violent war. You cannot have mercy on sin, you have to utterly destroy it, or sin will destroy you. Cling to your sword and shield as though you were clinging unto your very life. God's strength and his Spirit keep us wielding the sword.

In order to conquer sin in your life, you need to put on the armor of God:

> *Wherefore take unto you the whole armour of God, that ye may be able to withstand in the evil day, and having done all, to stand. Stand therefore, having your loins girt about with truth, and having on the breastplate of righteousness; and your feet shod with the preparation of the gospel of peace; Above all, taking the shield of faith, wherewith ye shall be able to quench all the fiery darts of the wicked. And take the helmet of salvation, and the sword of the Spirit, which is the word of God.*
>
> —Eph. 6:13–17

The warrior is a sight to behold as though he came from a different world. All he knows is war. All he knows is his armor and weapons. All he does is practice all day long, for soon his life will depend on his knowledge of his weapons and his skill. His mind is not unstable but prepared for action. In his heart there is no mercy for the enemy. The enemy must be utterly destroyed. There can be no second thoughts about it. "For the weapons of our warfare are not carnal, but mighty through God to the pulling down of strongholds" (2 Cor. 10:4).

It is time for you to put on the armor of God and walk into battle. The enemy has lifted up his voice and has defied the army of God. Will you allow him to continue to mock God's Spirit in your life?

> *Dearly beloved, I beseech you as strangers and pilgrims, abstain from fleshly lusts, which war against the soul.*
>
> —1 Pet. 2:11

> *But I see another law in my members, warring against the law of my mind, and bringing me into captivity to the law of sin which is in my members.*
>
> —Rom. 7:23

> *From whence come wars and fightings among you? Come they not hence, even of your lusts that war in your members?*
>
> —Jas. 4:1

The battle is over our souls, and the battleground is in our souls.

Do you know who the real enemy is? You think Satan is the real enemy? Satan is already a defeated foe. If it wasn't for Satan, I would be bored in the ministry. It is always an adventure and a challenge to find his lies and expose him. The only thing he can do is deceive you that God and his

Word are lies. That is all his strategy. There is another enemy who holds a lot of weight and power over you. Jesus knew who the real enemy was. He told you to deny him and crucify him. The real enemy is the only one who can stop you from obtaining eternal life. The real enemy is yourself.

You are the only one who limits the truth of God's Word in your life. You are the only one who decides to accept Jesus Christ or reject him. You are the only one who decides to walk in God's ways or not. You are the only one who decides to pray or not. You are the only one who convinces yourself of what is true.

Inside of all of us there is a mighty spiritual war—a war between choosing good or choosing evil. We choose to submit to our emotions, or we choose to fight our soul and submit to God. Our hearts are where all the goodness or all the evil in the world has come from. We are all capable of such goodness, and we are all capable of such horrors.

God has called us to bring an end to the evil within us. This is your destiny. This is your purpose on earth, and yet it is only the beginning. Once you climb over this wall, God will show you the rest of your life, one day at a time.

Your enemy is your thoughts, your habits, your emotions, your attitudes, and your fleshly desires. This is what we know as our soul, our flesh. Our inner man (spirit man) desires to do the will of the Father, but the soul and flesh have their own desires.

The war for our soul is fought in our minds. We fight one thought at a time. If you entertain evil thoughts, they will open a spiritual door for evil spiritual forces to come into your life. ". . . giving heed to seducing spirits . . ." (1 Tim. 4:1).

Our struggle is not against people, our fellow employees, our spouse or family members, or our neighbors. *Our struggle is against our thoughts.* It is a spiritual struggle. There in the doorway of our thoughts is where obedience or sin is born. Established thoughts then usher in seducing spirits or the Holy Spirit—torment and fear or joy, peace, and love.

Rise up in the grace of God and bring every thought to the feet of Jesus Christ. You are called to be a warrior and renew your mind with the truth. Rise up, and fight. Do not have self-pity. Don't be a coward. Stand up and fight, Soldier. Stop giving in to your emotional thoughts. They make you weak. You are called to be strong in God's Spirit. People of great inner peace and meekness are spiritually violent people.

What do we do with our fleshly desires? What the Bible says: crucify the flesh and consider ourselves dead unto sin. We need power from on high to say no to the voice of the flesh, but the flesh shall fall one thought at a time. The voice of the flesh may be strong in your life. That is about to change by the power and grace of God. Bring one thought at a time to Jesus, and soon the flesh will lose its power over you.

How can you say that you have the victory, if you have not gone to battle? You cannot just mentally believe that you are the righteousness of God. You must go out to battle and be victorious in Christ Jesus. Go out and possess the promises of God with spiritual violence. Go to battle, cut off the head of your Goliath, and raise his head for everyone to see. Praise God, and cry out, "See, my God is real! See, my God is alive in me! He has made me more than a conqueror!"

The trumpet for war has sounded. A shout of war has been declared. God is in the battlefield. Where are you? Don't you know that there is a war going on over the destiny of your soul?

Now, let's take this one step at a time. Your job is to be a warrior for God. Your only true enemy is yourself. The Word of God says to bring captive every thought to the obedience of Jesus Christ (2 Cor. 10:5). You are called to war against your soul. ". . . abstain from fleshly lusts, which war against the soul" (1 Pet. 2:11).

Bringing every thought to the obedience of Christ requires spiritual stamina. You must bring captive every thought. The word *captive* demands violence or spiritual warfare within your soul. To obey God's thoughts over your thoughts requires a humble heart, a contrite spirit, and a brokenness of one's own will. To have this attitude, you have to be spiritually violent and be convinced that bringing your soul captive to Christ is your only solution. Have you reached that level yet?

"And having in a readiness to avenge all disobedience when your obedience is fulfilled" (2 Cor. 10:6). People either live in fulfilled obedience, or they are still living in vain imaginations.

When people become prisoners of their souls, their bodies suffer because of their thoughts. Most people are prisoners of their minds and emotions. Many of them suffer mental disorders and emotional distress because they do not understand how to be a warrior for God.

You do not have to be a slave to your emotions. You do not have to be a slave to depression. You do not have to give in to every emotion that comes to you. You do not have to succumb to every desire of your body. You do not have to listen to every crazy thought that comes into your mind.

Do not give in to reason, emotions, or desires. Do not go after the flesh, but go after the Spirit (Rom. 8:1). Stop giving in to the flesh because the flesh can never be satisfied. Flesh is only flesh, and it is temporal. There is no glory, power, or real satisfaction in the flesh, just the law of sin and death. We are more than mere flesh, we are made in the image of God

Instead, submit to the Spirit. Understand that you have a God. He has offered you his power for your benefit. There is power from God for you to take every thought captive and bring it to the obedience of Jesus Christ. This is one major reason why God provides his power, strength, and grace for you. There is so much power in God, and it is available for you. Take his power and bring every thought captive to the obedience of Jesus Christ.

Speaking in tongues is not true power. Dancing in church is not power. Shouting in church is not power. True power is given to us, so we can capture our thoughts and bring them to the obedience of Jesus Christ. That is power. If Christians cannot submit their souls to Jesus, they have no power in their lives but only religion. Without this power in us to bring captive every thought to the obedience to Jesus Christ, there will never be a true relationship with

God. There will never be a spiritual change in our lives, and we will never experience what it is to move from glory to glory.

Mental institutions are full of people who do not know how to war against their thoughts. They have no inner strength to take a thought captive to God because they do not know God. Hospitals have to treat countless people with venereal diseases because they do not have the spiritual knowledge and spiritual weapons to overcome their flesh. Our jails are full of murderers, thieves, and rapists. Many of them claim to hear satanic voices telling them to commit these crimes. They could not resist because they did not know how.

I cannot overemphasize the importance of bringing every thought captive to the obedience of Jesus Christ. Second Corinthians 10:5 was not written by me or by man but by the Holy Spirit. This is God telling us to bring every thought to the obedience of Jesus Christ. Do not take it lightly. Rise up in the name of Jesus, and do it.

Every time you bring a thought captive, you are breaking strongholds in your life. These strongholds are attitudes that have formed because you didn't know God. These strongholds keep you bitter, offended, fearful, confused, poor, wretched, and bound. Now that you know God and his ways, those strongholds will come down in the name of Jesus, one thought at a time.

Strongholds are also mental attitudes that have been formed by your opinions, criticisms, and arguments. These attitudes are the reason you do not seek after and submit to God. These attitudes and arguments must come down in the name of Jesus, one thought at a time.

Strongholds are what keep people from obeying the truth. They are weights that keep people's spirits from freely walking on the water. These strongholds also keep people from experiencing the reality of God in their lives. "Let us lay aside every weight, and the sin which doth so easily beset us, and let us run with patience the race that is set before us . . ." (Heb. 12:1).

Do you want to experience his power? It is here now, and it is available. Therefore, with God's power, take every thought captive and bring it to the obedience of Jesus Christ. You will understand like never before that it is a privilege to be a son of God. Run to the battle, and Goliath will fall before you.

When you begin to obey God and submit one thought at a time, all the powers of hell will come against you. They will try everything in their power to stop you from obeying God. They will try every deception to lead you astray. But no power in hell can stop the grace of God from empowering a willing heart to obey truth.

Soon you will look at the people like Elijah saw the prophets of Baal. You will laugh and say, "Where is your god? Is he sleeping?" Where is the god of this world? Is it money? Can money save you from death? When you are lying on the bed of some incurable disease, can money help you, then? For all of those intellectuals who made wisdom and ego their god, can their god help them when they stand before God?

The gods of this world are money, power, beauty, physical strength, and people's own intellects. With all their gods, they crumble when God shakes their foundation. There is no inner strength, inner peace, or inner beauty in them. These things are for those who put on the armor of God and go into battle. These things are for those who love God and are warriors of God's Spirit.

Can you begin to see the difference between those who are warriors of God and those who are not? The ones who aren't are victims of circumstances and always react to circumstances. Their inner strength depends on everything going their way. However, life is meant for us to learn to trust in God and not in ourselves.

Take a look at the famous and rich people. They are beautiful and talented, rich and powerful, but they are full of themselves. The teaching of Jesus Christ is to deny yourself and think of your neighbor first. Because these famous people are full of themselves, they cannot cope with life. Still, they are in God's world, and God will shake their foundation.

People without the knowledge of God's ways have no inner peace or strength. They are constantly searching for self-empowerment. Just watch them. They may have it all materially, but spiritually they are lost.

God has called us to be a spiritual people who are led by his Spirit. The world does not have God, therefore worldly people can never be spiritual. What type of people are they? Carnal. Emotional. Intellectual. Beloved, we are called to live on a higher plane, a spiritual plane.

Every time I go out, I watch people. They are prisoners of their souls. I can see fear, hopelessness, confusion, and despair in their eyes. They place all their trust in money and despise people who take their things. They are empty. Life has become a weight around their necks. Life has become meaningless because without God there is no reason to exist. They have no life in them because the Spirit of life is far from their hearts. They are walking zombies, just trying to get by until they die.

Jesus said, "Come unto me, all ye that labour and are heavy laden, and I will give you rest. Take my yoke upon you, and learn of me; for I am meek and lowly in heart: and ye shall find rest unto your souls. For my yoke is easy, and my burden is light" (Matt. 11:28–30).

How do you renew your mind? How do you purify your soul? How do you love the Lord with all your soul? How do you take the kingdom of God by force? How do you go after the Spirit? How do you obey God's Word? How do you live victoriously and in the power of God? How do you walk in holiness? By bringing one thought at a time to the obedience of Jesus Christ. Nothing in the world is more important than this.

Once you start this process, you never give up or stop. Tell your emotions that you are never going to quit. Make up your mind that you are never going back to your old lifestyle. Commit like you never committed before. Let your will reach a new horizon. Tell yourself that you are going forward and forward, come hell and high water, you are going forward and higher until you reach heaven. Announce it to the host of heaven and to the demons in hell that you are not a coward. You are God's child and valiant unto death.

Say like men of old,

> *I have fought a good fight, I have finished my course, I have kept the faith: henceforth there is laid up for me a crown of righteousness, which the Lord, the righteous judge, shall give me at that day: and not to me only, but unto all them also that love his appearing.*
>
> —2 Tim. 4:7–8

> *Now the just shall live by faith: but if any man draw back, my soul shall have no pleasure in him But we are not of them who draw back unto perdition; but of them that believe to the saving of the soul.*
>
> —Heb. 10:38–39

The kingdom of God suffers violence, and the violent take it by force. I see a violent spiritual people who refuse to be in bondage to Satan, to their souls, or to their fleshly desires. I see an army of Christians rising up in the power and might of God. I see them pulling down the strongholds of the enemy. I see them climbing over the walls that kept them the prisoners of sin. I see them taking back the city that the enemy stole which is their lives. All prophecy is coming together. The world will stand back in awe as Christians rise up and allow their lights to shine.

> *Blow ye the trumpet in Zion, and sound an alarm in my holy mountain: let all the inhabitants of the land tremble: for the day of the Lord cometh, for it is nigh at hand . . . a great people and a strong; there hath not been ever the like, neither shall be any more after it, even to the years of many generations . . . nothing will escape them . . . as a strong people set in battle array . . .*

> *They shall run like mighty men; they shall climb the wall like men of war; and they shall march every one on his ways . . . they shall walk every one in his path: and when they shall fall upon a sword, they shall not be wounded . . . the earth shall quake before them. . . . And the Lord shall utter his voice before his army: for his camp is very great: for he is strong that executeth his word: for the day of the Lord is great and very terrible; and who can abide it.*
>
> —Joel 2:1–11

The Outcome of War

War is not always the way of life for God's people. After Israel invaded Jericho and conquered they became established in the land. The result of war is to establish oneself in a new land or a new promise. God wants an established people unto himself (Deut. 29:13).

> *To the end he may establish your hearts unblamable in holiness before God, even our Father, at the coming of our Lord Jesus Christ with all his saints.*
>
> —1 Thess. 3:13

> *But the Lord is faithful, who shall stablish you, and keep you from evil.*
>
> —2 Thess. 3:3

If your heart is not established, it is because you have not gone out to war. If you have not gone out to war, you are still mastered by evil.

> *Know ye not, that to whom ye yield yourselves servants to obey, his servants ye are to whom ye obey, whether of sin*

> *unto death, or of obedience unto righteousness? But God be thanked that ye were servants of sin but ye have obeyed from the heart that form of doctrine which was delivered you.*
> —Rom. 6:16–17

An established heart in the Lord is another trait that we can have in common with the apostles. The apostles' hearts were established in the truth. They were so established that even in their dreams they saw themselves doing the will of the Father. Our hearts must be established on the rock, which is Christ, and on his gospel, which is the truth and power. "Rooted and built up in him, and established in the faith, as ye have been taught, abounding therein with thanksgiving" (Col. 2:7).

We must be established so that the truth of God's Word could govern our hearts. If our hearts are not established in truth, we could easily be tossed to and fro by anything. If our hearts are not established, Christianity is impossible to obey. If our hearts are not established, our thoughts, emotions and fleshly desires dictate our lifestyles to us. Therefore, become established.

Make up your mind once and for all that you are going to obey God's Word, no matter the cost. Enter into war for control of your soul. Let us conquer our souls so that we can go on with the things of God. The difference between you and a new convert of the faith will be that you are established on the Word of the living God. Therefore, you are no longer moved by emotions, reasons, or desires. You have become a warrior in the Spirit. You have become God's untouchable. You have become a demon slayer.

He shall not be afraid of evil tidings, his heart is fixed, trusting in the Lord. His heart is established, he shall not be afraid, until he see his desire upon his enemies.

—Ps. 112:7–8

Chapter 10

WALKING IN NEWNESS OF LIFE

Therefore we are buried with him by baptism into death: that like as Christ was raised up from the dead by the glory of the Father, even so we also should walk in newness of life.

—Rom. 6:4

You have come to the final chapter and now you have gained knowledge of eternal things that few in the history of mankind have ever read. It is a privilege to know what you know. You have read the secrets of life and how to walk on water. However, spiritually you are not ready because you only have knowledge.

Knowledge becomes wisdom when you apply knowledge to your life. Then you will be wise, but now you only know theories. God desires to establish your heart in these spiritual truths through fire. It would be a shame to know how to walk on water, and yet never step out of the boat.

If you are going through a trial right now, you must realize that God is working better truth, grace, anointing, wisdom, and power in your life. Not many Christians are capable of understanding such a concept. You must discipline yourself to focus on Jesus and not on people or circumstances. Allow God's Spirit to have his way in your life and completely trust in his wisdom and power.

When you fight in the natural using your emotions, your wisdom, or physical violence, you resist God's way of working in your life. You focus on the natural and not on the supernatural. You alone must learn how to be still in God, to rest from your own works, and allow God to be God in your life.

> *Looking unto Jesus the author and finisher of our faith; who for the joy that was set before him endured the cross, despising the shame, and is set down at the right hand of the throne of God. For consider him that endured such contradiction of sinners against himself, lest ye be wearied and faint in your minds. Ye have not yet resisted unto blood, striving against sin.*
>
> —Heb. 12:2–4

You have read this book and analyzed it with your reason, and you have made your own conclusions. That is how we all approach life. If what you read is true, it will prevail. In time, God will bring you to greater depths of knowledge, understanding, and a relationship with his Spirit. After reading this book, please return to the beginning and read it again and again until you've gained revelation knowledge.

Every day is a new day with the opportunity for a new beginning. Every day is a gift from God. Every day is unique because it was created only once. It will never be again. Every day let the Word of God be a lamp unto your feet (Ps. 119:105).

The Word of God is a spiritual book. The Bible is the Word of God. There is none like it. All the mysteries of life are explained in the Bible. The reason you exist and how you should live your life are explained in the Bible. Your beginning and your ending are described in the Bible.

Whatever has kept you from pursuing the study of the Bible falls squarely on your own shoulders. Only you will be held accountable for your life. The awesome thing about Christianity is that our relationship with God does not depend on circumstances or on someone but simply on ourselves. No one can save you but God. No one will judge you but God. Therefore, adverse circumstances and people provide an opportunity for you to obey God and receive blessings. Do not allow those opportunities to pass you by. Grab hold of God, and grab hold of the cross.

Christianity is a personal relationship with God. You only mature when you stop asking God to change you and begin to war against your soul. The beauty about Christianity is that it is custom-made for every individual. God challenges you to know him and not resist his Spirit in your life. Where ever you find yourself, humble yourself, and obey God.

In God's wisdom, he has prepared everything. He has planned everything. God has made preparations for a great feast at the end of time for believers who have learned and lived by his ways, also known as his church, the Bride.

God has also prepared torment and the lake of fire for Satan and his perverted angels. You are not predestined to join the Devil. You are predestined to join Jesus at the great feast. The only thing that will keep you from heaven is your lack of spiritual interest.

There are only two predestinations for every individual. There are only two ways of living life. There are only two types of walks. There are only two choices. There are only two types of people—those who know the truth and those who are deceived, or between those who have reprobate minds and those who are renewing their minds.

There are only two types of vessels. One vessel has been predestined for glory and the other for wrath. Whether you like it or not, you are living a predestined life. Everything about you, your whole being and your whole life are already known. It is your responsibility to seek spiritual knowledge.

If you do not obtain knowledge, how will you grow in wisdom to walk in newness of life? If you do not grow in wisdom, how can you fulfill your destiny on earth?

God incarnate, Jesus Christ dwelled among us. He came from another kingdom to enlighten us so that we can have abundant life. He came to preach and teach a new way. He called it the gospel of the kingdom (Mark 1:14; Luke 4:43). It is the good news of the kingdom of God (Luke 8:1).

In order to grasp the meaning of newness of life in Jesus Christ, we must be able to grasp his teachings and apply them to our lives. The gospel of the kingdom of heaven deals with the condition of the heart. It deals with attitudes and perspectives.

On one occasion, a scribe commented that loving God and loving his neighbor had more spiritual value than burnt offerings and sacrifices. Jesus saw that the scribe answered wisely and replied, ". . . thou are not far from the kingdom of God" (Mark 12:33–34). Such is the case of many people who stand on the brink of eternity.

Jesus Christ prophesied that the gospel of the kingdom would be preached to all the world as a witness unto all the nations and then the end would come (Matt. 24:14). Jesus Christ has made it very clear that the message of the kingdom of heaven will reach the ears of many people. However, it is up to the individual to accept or reject this message. "Even the very dust of your city, which cleaveth on us, we do wipe off against you: notwithstanding be sure of this, that the kingdom of God is come nigh unto you" (Luke 10:11).

God gave men the ability to understand spiritual truth and with the invention of television, movies, radio, satellite, and the Internet, the gospel of the kingdom is reaching millions of people like never in the history of mankind. Before our very eyes, this prophecy of Jesus is being fulfilled.

Jesus Christ has predetermined that we must seek first the kingdom of God (Matt. 6:33). The reason is simple: our everlasting eternity hinges on our being able to grasp the spiritual meaning of the kingdom of heaven. There is nothing in this present world more important than growing in the wisdom of the kingdom of God. "There shall be weeping and gnashing of teeth, when ye shall see Abraham, and Isaac, and Jacob, and all the prophets, in the kingdom of God, and you yourselves thrust out" (Luke 13:28).

In order to receive the kingdom of God we must have the attitude of a child who is willing to learn, trust, accept, and grow. "Verily I say unto you, Whosoever shall not receive the kingdom of God as a little child shall in no wise enter therein" (Luke 18:17).

The kingdom of God is not a complicated concept. The understanding of the mysteries of the kingdom has been given unto us (Luke 8:10). "Fear not little flock; for it is your Father's good pleasure to give you the kingdom" (Luke 12:32).

The kingdom of God is much more than knowing that we are going to heaven. The true understanding of the kingdom is allowing the kingdom of Jesus to overrun our lives. It is the desire of God that we live in this present life with heaven inside of us. In other words, we do not have to reach heaven to experience what heaven is like. We can ascertain heaven or the kingdom of God right now, here on earth, inside our being.

"Neither shall they say, lo here! Or, lo there! For, behold, the kingdom of God is within you" (Luke 17:21). "For the kingdom of God is not meat or drink; but righteousness, and peace, and joy in the Holy Ghost" (Rom. 14:17). "For the kingdom of God is not in word but in power" (1 Cor. 4:20). Newness of life is obtaining that level in the Holy Spirit whereby we walk on earth with heaven abiding and flowing through us. This coincides with the teachings of the New Testament in that we are in Christ and we do things through and by Christ and his Spirit.

Jesus Christ taught, "Verily, verily, I say unto thee, Except a man be born of water and of the Spirit, he cannot enter into the kingdom of God. That which is born of the flesh is flesh; and that which is born of the Spirit is spirit. Marvel not that I said unto thee, Ye must be born again" (John 3:5–7).

The meaning of such verses is profound beyond our imagination. If we could only grasp what Jesus Christ is trying to convey to our hearts, we would begin to see life through new eyes. We are born of God, oh, the spiritual depth of such knowledge! Let us drink of such knowledge. Let us be filled with the Spirit of God. Let us have a new life from God. Let us be a new creature who lives in the world yet is not of the world but is born and partakes of another world (John 15:19, 17:14–16).

We are born again by believing in Jesus Christ. We are born into a faith world, a spiritual world (John 3:15–18). A new life of light is set before us by the power of God (John 1:12). "Giving thanks unto the Father, which hath made us meet to be partakers of the inheritance of the saints in light: Who hath delivered us from the power of darkness, and hath translated us into the kingdom of his dear Son" (Col. 1:12–13).

We are born again into a kingdom of light. No darkness or evil will inherit the kingdom of God (1 Cor. 6:10; Gal. 5:21; Eph. 5:5). Jesus Christ taught that we are born into his kingdom by faith, but in order to remain there we must also be born of water.

Water is symbolic of washing which means that if we obey the truth it will wash our souls. "For everyone that doeth evil hateth the light, neither cometh to the light, lest his deeds should be reproved. But he that doeth truth cometh to the light, that his deeds may be made manifest, that they are wrought in God" (John 3:20–21).

This whole book is dedicated to giving you knowledge about exactly how to wash your soul and be established in truth and in the kingdom of God. If you practice exactly what you have read in this book, soon the kingdom of God will reside in you. Light will come into your being. You will see life through a different viewpoint and live life with a different attitude.

Washing our souls with the truth is the challenge set before all Christians. This process is also known as, "For the perfecting of the saints, for the work of the ministry, for the edifying of the body of Christ: Till we all come in the unity of the faith, and of the knowledge of the Son of God, unto a perfect man, unto the measure of the stature of the fulness of Christ" (Eph. 4:12–13).

A Christian is taught to always obtain some type of excellence. It is my desire that you understand exactly what that is and how to accomplish this goal. It is simply submitting our souls to Christ as prescribed in previous chapters. When we are born again, we continue to wash our souls with the truth, and we grow in the light of the kingdom of God.

The New Testament speaks of this process of submitting our souls as growing. "As newborn babes, desire the sincere milk of the word, that ye may grow thereby" (1 Pet. 2:2). We are called to grow in grace and in knowledge (2 Pet. 3:18). We need to grow in faith (2 Thess. 1:3). We need to speak the truth in love and grow up into Christ (Eph. 4:15).

The New Testament describes us as a building growing or being edified together in the likeness of Christ (Eph. 2:21, 4:16). When we obey Christ and wash our souls with his word, we are being perfected in Christ. We are re-formed to be like Christ.

It is our souls that keep us from walking on water. We are constantly reacting with our soul to the natural. We are led by the natural which is our intellect and emotions. However, we are called to be led by the Spirit of truth and not by our souls. Our souls were given to us so we could experience the beauty and awe of God abiding in us.

Our purpose on earth is to accept Jesus Christ as our Lord and Savior. With this simple act of confession, if we die on the spot, we have access to heaven. However, if we will live out our lives, we need to wash our souls by obeying the truth.

Every soul has been predestined to be broken in order to obey God's truth. However, if any soul is incapable of understanding such spiritual truths, he has no part in the things of God. Jesus declared, "Whosoever shall fall on this stone shall be broken: but on whomsoever it shall fall, it will grind him to powder" (Matt. 21:44).

When we reach that place in Christ by experiencing trials and tribulations, we no longer react from our soul but from our spirit that has been established in faith, hope, and love. That is where the teachings of Christ and the Holy Spirit lead and guide us. A soul that has been disciplined and governed by the Spirit is a mature spiritual being.

For whom the Lord loveth he chasteneth, and scourgeth every son whom he receiveth. If ye endure chastening, God dealeth

> *with you as with sons; for what son is he whom the father chasteneth not? But if ye be without chastisement, whereof all are partakers, then are ye bastards, and not sons.*
>
> —Heb. 12:6–8

After warring and submitting our souls to Christ, we become disciplined and chaste ministers. This process is refined through fire. Trials and tribulations cause our souls to react. We have reached a wonderful place in the Spirit when our emotions no longer burst out, but only obedience of the Word flows from inside us. Then you will be a disciplined being, spirit-controlled character.

This is the attitude of individuals who allow God to work in their lives:

> *Giving no offence in anything, that the ministry be not blamed: but in all things approving ourselves as the ministers of God, in much patience, in afflictions, in necessities, in distresses, in stripes, in imprisonments, in tumults, in labours, in watchings, in fastings; by pureness, by knowledge, by longsuffering, by kindness, by the Holy Ghost, by love unfeigned, by the word of truth, by the power of God, by the armour of righteousness on the right hand and on the left, by honour and dishonour, by evil report and good report: as deceivers, and yet true; as unknown, and yet well known; as dying, and, behold, we live; as chastened, and not killed; as sorrowful, yet always rejoicing; as poor, yet making many rich; as having nothing, and yet possessing all things".*
>
> —2 Cor. 6:3–10

A chastened person is one who no longer has the luxury of being emotional, giving in to anger, or submitting to hurt feelings. A scourged Christian no longer has the privilege of being offended or giving in to offense. The only privilege a chastened person has is giving in to a broken heart and being led by the Spirit to the cross.

A disciplined person respects everyone's point of view and inwardly understands that the answer is not in arguments. The answer is in being or not being. First, being a disciple of God that you may learn spiritual truths. First, gain spiritual knowledge then practice that knowledge. With time, the anointing comes to make you a blessed individual.

Doctrine and theology are very important because they set a correct path. However, knowledge of theology without obedience is only vain religion. Knowledge with obedience is a relationship with God. Knowledge is not the final goal of a Christian but an established heart through obedience.

The Bible teaches that knowledge without love only produces pride (1 Cor. 8:1). The things of God are not about how much you know but how much your spirit, soul, and body are submitted to God. True spirituality is not about knowledge or debating theological points of view. Once again, true spirituality is yielding your will in obedience to the Word of God.

> *As ye have therefore received Christ Jesus the Lord, so walk ye in him: Rooted and built up in him, and stablished in the faith, as ye have been taught, abounding therein with thanksgiving. Beware lest any man spoil you through philosophy and vain deceit, after the tradition of men, after the rudiments of the world, and not after Christ.*
>
> —Col. 2:6–8

> *O Timothy, keep that which is committed to thy trust, avoiding profane and vain babblings, and oppositions of science falsely so called: Which some professing have erred concerning the faith.*
>
> —1 Tim. 6:20–21

It takes wisdom in spiritual things and complete dedication to simply yield your life to God. Not many people can or know how to submit. Those who rise through the ranks enjoy an abundant spiritual life.

The church has accumulated theological knowledge but does not know what to do with it. The church has gained knowledge on many theological points of view but the Spirit has brought up spiritual hunger that has caused unrest in the church. The church stands at the crossroads and does not know its next step. The church is waiting for new five-fold spiritual ministers to show the way. They are the new wineskins that hold new attitudes. There is a spiritual change of the guards on the watchtowers of our souls. You, My Dear Reader, are called to be such a minister and guide the church in such a way.

What is that way? ". . . and yet shew I unto you a more excellent way" (1 Cor. 12:31). This is the introduction of the Holy Spirit to a mighty spiritual chapter. A chapter that will live for eternity. A chapter that did not come from the heart of men but from the heart of God. A chapter like no other, found no other place but in the word of God. The mighty chapter of 1 Corinthians 13, the chapter of love and true spirituality. Whoever has spiritual ears listen to what you are about to read.

> *Though I speak with the tongues of men and of angels, and have not love, I am become as sounding brass, or a tinkling cymbal. And though I have the gift of prophecy, and understand all mysteries, and all knowledge; and though I have all faith, so that I could remove mountains, and have no love, I am nothing. And though I bestow all my goods to feed the poor, and though I give my body to be burned, and have not charity, it profiteth me nothing.*
>
> —1 Cor. 13:1–3

These first three verses are given to us as a precaution against becoming religious. It warns us that our goal in life is not simply to speak in tongues, or move mountains by faith, or give all our money away. The Spirit of God is trying to give us understanding that there is a higher level that we must reach.

I am amazed at the wisdom of God's Word. God knew that in our time, the church would be stuck exactly in these three verses. However, the Spirit of God wants us to be led by the Spirit and walk into the excellent way. What is love and what is the excellent way? The next five verses tell us exactly what it is.

> *Love suffereth long, and is kind; love envieth not; love vaunteth not itself, is not puffed up, Doth not behave itself unseemly, seeketh not her own, is not easily provoked, thinketh no evil; Rejoiceth not in iniquity, but rejoiceth in the truth; Beareth all things, believeth all things, hopeth all things, endureth all things. Love never faileth: but whether there be prophecies, they shall fail; whether there be tongues, they shall cease; whether there be knowledge, it shall vanish away.*
>
> —1 Cor. 13:4–8

Love will never vanish or fail. If there is unconditional love in your heart for your spouse, your marriage will never fail. If there is unconditional love for your congregation, your ministry will never fail. If you learn to walk in unconditional love, you will never fail. If you learn to walk in unconditional love you will experience heaven in your heart.

When we stand before God, our deeds will be tried by fire. The only works that will remain and are not consumed are our deeds done in love (1 Cor. 3:13–15). When we stand before God, he will not care how much theology we know but only if we yielded to his Spirit and bore fruit, especially the fruit of love.

> *For we know in part, and we prophesy in part. But when that which is perfect is come, then that which is in part shall be done away. When I was a child, I spake as a child, I understood as a child, I thought as a child: but when I became a man, I put away childish things. For now we see through a glass, darkly; but then face to face: now I know in part; but then shall I know even as also I am known.*
>
> —1 Cor. 13:9–12

Are you ready to put away childish things? God sees humanity as children who constantly fight for temporal things. A child only understands selfishness. He thinks and acts in selfishness. It is time to grow up and be mature in the Spirit of God for that which is perfect in love is coming.

A father cannot trust a child with power. The child will only abuse such a power for his own unscrupulous, selfish desires. The father will only trust the child with his power when the child has grown in discipline and wisdom. We are destined to live and walk in great power. The father is waiting to bestow his power upon scourged disciples.

The day is coming when we shall stand before this perfect God of love. Now, we simply understand in part but we do not have complete four-dimensional experience. However, when we stand before him and behold his radiance face to face, then shall we know as we are known.

In other words, everything about us is now known. There is nothing that can be kept secret from this awesome Spirit of love—nothing! Every thought, intention, motive, feeling, desire, act in our hearts, is known. However, we ourselves do not fully understand or know exactly what is coming. One day, though, we will.

In heaven, there is only one language, the universal language of love. In heaven there is no need to speak because who we are is transmitted. We are known by what we transmit. Jesus said, "By this shall all men know that ye are my disciples, if ye have love one to another" (John 13:35).

This God of love is coming. In him there is no variance or evil because his love cannot allow it. His love has conquered all evil and all darkness. There is no weakness in his love. There is a power in love beyond our imaginations. He is God because he is love. Love is supreme and all powerful.

As this holy God of love comes near us on that day when we stand before him, as his pure love approaches our spirit, our conscience will cry out. "Please, Jesus, don't come any closer. I can't bear it!" If we did not prepare our lives for such a day, and we lived with selfishness and never learned to love, that day will be intolerable.

"Please God, do not come any nearer. You are pure, and I cannot stand in your presence. The closer you draw, the dirtier I feel, and I can't bear it. I can't bear to stand in your light." Then shall there be weeping and gnashing of teeth. The teachings of Jesus Christ warn us of such a day. His teachings also prepare us for such a day.

1 Corinthians 13:13, the final verse of this chapter reads: "And now abideth faith, hope, love, these three; but the greatest of these is love."

In the end, the only thing that matters is if you allow Jesus Christ to establish faith, hope, and love in your heart. Nothing else will last, not denominations, nations, governments, or galaxies. If the Bible says that only faith, hope, and love will abide, then these three words must have a high importance in our lives.

How important are these three words? They are so important that everything that exists comes from these words. Everything in the Bible points to these three words. These words are our origin and our final destination.

The kingdom of God is a spiritual kingdom. His kingdom is composed of faith, hope, and love. These three simple words that cannot be seen, yet life is composed of such words. We are called to abound in these words for in them we find the kingdom of heaven.

Walking in newness of life is walking or growing in faith, hope, and love. Walking in faith is simply being established in the truth of God's Word. When a problem arises, faith in God's Word arises in our hearts to combat the problem. The problem doesn't matter because faith in God's Word changes all things. Faith in God's Word changes physical circumstances. Before the problem even arises, the answer has already been provided in the Word of God.

Has such a faith been established in your relationship with the Almighty One and his Word? Are you ready for this type of Christianity? Are you ready to come out of the boat? You don't know what you are missing!

Walking in hope is growing in hope, which is prescribed in Chapter Two. Hope is the understanding that our days are numbered on earth, and soon we will stand in judgment. If we grow in the hope, we will change our lifestyles.

Hope also orientates our faith toward a more godly and spiritual use. Established hope in our heart drives us to do something worthwhile on earth for God and not just live for selfish reasons. If we live only once, then let our lives count for the kingdom of God!

Walking in unconditional love is the highest spiritual level. Once you reached this level, you are walking on water. This is the level that Jesus obtained and showed us the way. On the cross he said, "Father, forgive them for they know not what they do."

Walking in love is also the level Stephen obtained. While he was being stoned to death he lovingly announced, "Lord, lay not this sin to their charge" (Acts 7:60). There is a deep spiritual knowledge in love. We are called to walk in love and be complete in Jesus and not harden or close our bowels of compassion (1 John 3:17).

Jesus and Stephen knew and understood the laws of the Spirit. They walked on earth and yet their hearts were established on spiritual truths. They knew a higher spiritual level than the soul.

Stephen reached that level by not resisting the Spirit or the ways of the Spirit. He tried to convey this understanding to religious people but theirs hearts could not understand spiritual concepts (Acts 7:51). Love was too deep and too high for them to comprehend.

Stephen reached that level in the Spirit where he experienced freedom from the dominion of the soul. Stephen was free in the Spirit and experienced the delight of walking on water. He enjoyed the freedom from fear, worry, anger, hate, vengeance, frustration, bitterness, and all negative emotions. His persecutors only knew the soul and were in bondage to their souls. Stephen had pity and compassion on them because he was free, and he knew they were not.

"And to know the love of Christ, which passeth knowledge, that ye might be filled with all the fulness of God" (Eph. 3:19).

Jesus Christ came to make a new life for us. He shed his blood for a new covenant (Matt. 26:28). He established a new commandment that we love one another as he loved us (John 13:34). The New Testament teaches to purge out the old leaven that we may be a new lump in Jesus Christ (1 Cor. 5:7). "Therefore if any man be in Christ, he is a new creature: old things are passed away; behold, all things are become new" (2 Cor. 5:17).

We exist to allow God to make a masterpiece out of a lump, to allow God to make a new creature from our hearts (Gal. 6:15). We are called to be a new type of species in which Christ is the first.

For whom he did foreknow, he also did predestinate to be conformed to the image of his Son, that he might be the firstborn among many brethren.

—Rom. 8:29

Of his own will begat he us with the word of truth, that we should be a kind of firstfruits of his creatures.

—Jas. 1:18

Having abolished in his flesh the enmity, even the law of commandments contained in ordinances; for to make in himself of twain one new man, so making peace.

—Eph. 2:15

And be renewed in the spirit of your mind; and that ye put on the new man, which after God is created in righteousness and true holiness.

—Eph. 4:23–24

And have put on the new man, which is renewed in knowledge after the image of him that created him . . . and above all these things put on love, which is the bond of perfectness.

—Col. 3:10,14

You are called to be conformed to the image of Christ. It is a beautiful image full of grace, light, and power. Christ has no fear, worry, or hate in his heart. His love conquers everything. His wisdom knows all things. He is not out to impress anyone; he only loves everyone. He is not trying to become anything. He is who he is, and he is at peace. He is the great "I am" (Ex. 3:14; John 8:58).

A Hidden Treasure

In the Gospels is an account of a woman who was in bondage to sin. She realized that her only salvation was Jesus Christ, so she began to seek him and to love him. When she found him, she fell at his feet and sobbed. She washed her tears from his feet with her hair. She then broke a vessel of costly perfume and anointed his feet.

When she broke the vessel of perfume, the precious aroma filled the room. The vessel carried such a wonderful aroma that everyone in the room was immediately awestruck. Everyone in the room realized it was a costly perfume.

Some ridiculed the action, but the aroma itself was beyond delight. Although some quarreled about the action, Jesus Christ delighted in her. Jesus responded to her action by declaring, "Thy sins are forgiven" (Luke 7:37–48).

There is a hidden treasure inside every Christian who has confessed Christ as Lord of their lives. If Christians place their lives in his hands and allow him to break this earthen vessel, his aroma will flow out for the world to enjoy. If Christians could allow him to break them, his Spirit or anointing will flow from their being. This anointing will heal their marriages and everyone who comes into contact with them.

God wants to create from your life a masterpiece in Christ. This is what God wants to do. Will you let him? Are you willing to allow God to break you and mold your life after him? Are you willing to be clay in his hands?

> *Even the mystery which hath been hid from ages and from generations, but now is made manifest to his saints: To whom God would make known what is the riches of the glory of this mystery among the Gentiles; which is Christ in you, the hope of glory.*
>
> —Col. 1:26–27

> *If any man thirst, let him come unto me, and drink. He that believeth on me, as the scripture hath said, out of his belly shall flow rivers of living water.*
>
> —John 7:37–38

> *The kingdom of heaven is like unto treasure hid in a field; the which when a man hath found, he hideth, and for joy thereof goeth and selleth all that he hath, and buyeth that field.*
>
> —Matt. 13:44

For people who do find the way of the kingdom, Jesus declares,

> *Come, ye blessed of my Father, inherit the kingdom prepared for you from the foundation of the world: for I was an hungered, and ye gave me meat: I was thirsty, and ye gave me drink: I was a stranger, and ye took me in: Naked, and ye clothed me: I was sick, and ye visited me: I was in prison, and ye came unto me.*
>
> —Matt. 25:34–36

There are no boundaries to our love except the boundaries we set up. The Spirit of God challenges us to step out of our boat of selfishness and into his love. The kingdom of

God has now come upon you (Luke 11:20). God's destiny is upon you. A new life in Christ awaits you.

> *If ye then be risen with Christ, seek those things which are above, where Christ sitteth on the right hand of God. Set your affection on things above, not on things on the earth. For ye are dead, and your life is hid with Christ in God.*
>
> —Col. 3:1–3

SOURCE

Vines Expository Dictionary (New York: Thomas Nelson, 1984).